Disrupting Silence

Kathleen Colantonio-Yurko / Brittany Adams (eds)

Disrupting Silence

Teaching and Learning about Rape Culture through Youth Texts

PETER LANG

New York · Berlin · Bruxelles · Chennai · Lausanne · Oxford

Library of Congress Cataloging-in-Publication Data
A CIP catalog record for this book has been applied for at the Library of Congress.
Names: Colantonio-Yurko, Kathleen, 1982- editor. | Adams, Brittany M., 1990- editor.
Title: Disrupting silence : teaching and learning about rape culture through youth texts / [edited by] Kathleen Colantonio-Yurko, Brittany Adams.
Description: New York : Peter Lang, [2025] | Includes bibliographical references.
Identifiers: LCCN 2024060059 (print) | LCCN 2024060060 (ebook) | ISBN 9781636675244 (paperback) | ISBN 9781636675251 (pdf) | ISBN 9781636675268 (epub)
Subjects: LCSH: Rape culture--Study and teaching (Secondary)--United States. | Rape culture in literature--Study and teaching (Secondary)
Classification: LCC HV6561 .D557 2025 (print) | LCC HV6561 (ebook) | DDC 362.88392071/273--dc23/eng/20250209
LC record available at https://lccn.loc.gov/2024060059
LC ebook record available at https://lccn.loc.gov/2024060060

Bibliographic Information published by the Deutsche Nationalbibliothek
The Deutsche Nationalbibliothek lists this publication in the Deutsche Nationalbibliografie; detailed bibliographic data is available in the internet at http://dnb.d-nb.de.

Cover image

© Bob Vector, iStock

Cover design by Peter Lang Group AG

ISBN 978-1-63667-524-4 (Print)
E-ISBN 978-1-63667-525-1 (E-PDF)
E-ISBN 978-1-63667-526-8 (E-PUB)
DOI 10.3726/b22669

© 2025 Peter Lang Group AG, Lausanne, Switzerland
Published by Peter Lang Publishing Inc., New York, USA

info@peterlang.com

All rights reserved.
All parts of this publication are protected by copyright. Any utilisation outside the strict limits of the copyright law, without the permission of the publisher, is forbidden and liable to prosecution. This applies in particular to reproductions, translations, microfilming, and storage and processing in electronic retrieval systems.

This publication has been peer reviewed.

www.peterlang.com

Contents

List of Tables   vii
Contributors   ix
Foreword   xi

Introduction 1

I. Making Space for Conversations about Rape Culture in Schools

Social Media as a Teachable Text: How Teachers Can Learn From and Use Social Media to Prepare for Discussions About Rape Culture 9
Molly C. Driessen

Sexual Assault in Young Adult Literature: Mirrors and Windows Into Experiences of Survivorship 27
Gillian E. Mertens

The Sharp Edge of Silence: Using a Young Adult Novel to C.A.R.E. For Students 45
Emily Pendergrass, Melanie Hundley, Michael Neel, and Kathryn Pendergrass

II. Critical Analysis of Youth Texts

"I want my entrance fee back": Institutional Betrayal in Young Adult Sexual Assault Narratives 61
Amber Moore and Elizabeth Marshall

Social, Communal, and Familial: Examining Isolation through Setting Analysis in Sexual Assault Young Adult Literature 83
Shelby Boehm, Henry Cody Miller, and Lorelei Starkey

Male Youth-Athletes as Victims of Sexual Violence in Recommended Sports-Related Young Adult Literature 95
Mark A. Lewis and Luke Rodesiler

III. Critical Understandings, Teaching, and Application

Disrupting Rape Myths and Objective Violence through Graphic Novels: A Critical Literacy Approach to Educating Emergent Bilingual Youth 109
Jie Y. Park

"It shouldn't take you personally knowing a potential victim to start being a decent person": Exploring the Importance of Vulnerability in Critical Literacy Learning 125
Brittany Adams

The Anti-Hero: Using Media Representations of Gendered Violence to Negotiate Rape Culture, Suicide Intensity, and Neoliberal Belonging 147
Cameron Greensmith, Adam Davies, and Jocelyn Sakal Froese

Notes on Contributors 161

List of Tables

2.1	Sample Text Themes and Survivorship Questions	38
5.1	Types of Isolation	87
5.2	Examples of Social Isolation	88
5.3	Examples of Communal Isolation	89
5.4	Examples of Familial Isolation	90
6.1	Selected Works of Sports-Related YAL Featuring a Male Victim of Sexual Violence	98

Contributors

Volume Editors:
Kathleen Colantonio-Yurko, State University of New York at Brockport
Brittany Adams, The University of Alabama

Foreword:
Ashley S. Boyd, Washington State University

Chapter Authors:
Brittany Adams, The University of Alabama
Shelby Boehm, Illinois State University
Adam Davies, University of Guelph in Guelph
Molly C. Driessen, Providence College
Cameron Greensmith, Kennesaw State University
Melanie Hundley, Vanderbilt University
Mark A. Lewis, James Madison University
Elizabeth A. Marshall, Simon Fraser University
Gillian E. Mertens, State University of New York at Cortland
Henry "Cody" Miller, State University of New York at Brockport
Amber Moore, The University of British Columbia
Michael Neel, Vanderbilt University
Jie Park, Clark University
Emily Pendergrass, Vanderbilt University
Kathryn Pendergrass, Lewis and Clark College
Luke Rodesiler, Purdue University Fort Wayne
Jocelyn Sakal Froese, Wilfrid Laurier University
Lorelei Starkey, Illinois State University

Foreword

From my own experiences teaching 9th grade English Language Arts for years, I have witnessed the misconceptions and lack of discussion around issues related to consent and rape culture. Often these topics are simplified for students, and young people are led to believe that a verbal "yes" is all that matters, when these issues are really much more complicated. Or, even worse, the topics are avoided altogether under the premise that they are too taboo for schools or that talking about them in some way engenders predatory behavior. I wish I had the text that follows in this volume as a burgeoning high school teacher who was concerned with the realities of my students' lives but who was unsure how to best approach them. The authors in this collection reject both the culture of silence that surrounds rape culture and the notion that teenagers are not equipped to understand complex and sensitive social issues.

For decades, scholars, teachers, and readers of young adult literature have heralded its potential for tackling sensitive topics. For instance, research has shown how students can develop complex understandings of bullying (Ryan & Hurst, 2021), disabilities (Darragh, 2015), and police brutality (Falter & Kerkoff, 2018) through reading and engaging with narratives written for youth. They can become more empathetic and aware (Ginsberg & Glenn, 2019) when they read narratives that both reflect their experiences and are invited to experience those of others. In 1999, the publication of Laurie Halse Anderson's *Speak*, a story about a teen girl's survival of a sexual assault early in her high school career and its aftermath, saw explosive popularity and proved the that the genre and its audiences were not only open to such topics but were also capable of confronting amongst them rape and rape culture. Since then, numerous authors have contributed to narratives around this topic (e.g. Reed, 2019; Yang, 2020), providing a multiplicity of perspectives and stories and defying a monolithic representation of assault and survival. And yet, secondary classroom spaces do not seem to have caught up to the openness and honesty of this literature. Why is this the case?

The editors and authors of this volume speak to this question, noting concerns around censorship, lack of teacher preparation, and fear. They offer myriad ways to address these limitations through pedagogical approaches that include engaging teachers and students with social media, establishing norms for difficult conversations, and providing content warnings prior to reading. Furthermore, they offer critical readings of texts that reflect youth's experiences as well as teach them about broader themes surrounding rape culture. This especially includes the role of institutions such as schools in perpetuating harm and protecting assailants. Their strategies and readings are insightful and timely as we continue in a political landscape wrought with attempts to thwart human rights and uphold cycles of privilege.

Furthermore, this collection advocates for a perception of youth as qualified to discuss rape culture with the criticality and sensitivity it deserves, and—just as important—as capable of enacting change. In her powerful memoir, *Know My Name*, Chanel Miller (2019) describes her assault by Stanford swimmer Brock Turner and tells her readers to: "'be the Swede,'" the men who interrupted Turner in the act and held him until authorities arrived. Miller writes, "Show up for the vulnerable, do your part, help each other and face the darkest parts alongside survivors." This book is an encouragement for all of us, but especially those of us who work as teachers, to do our part in eradicating the insidious existence of rape culture and to build a justice-oriented citizenry grounded in respect for all humans.

– Ashley S. Boyd
Professor of English Education
Washington State University

References

Anderson, L. H. (1999). *Speak*. Square Fish.

Darragh, J. J., & Radmer, E. (2016). Connecting to their lives: Young adult literature and student achievement. *Making Literacy Connections*, 31, 18-31.

Falter, M. M., & Kerkhoff, S. N. (2018). Slowly shifting out of neutral: Using young adult literature to discuss PSTs' beliefs about racial injustice and police brutality. *English Teaching: Practice & Critique*, 17(3), 257-276.

Ginsberg, R. & Glenn, W. J. (2019). Moments of pause: Understanding students' shifting perceptions during a Muslim young adult literature learning experience. *Reading Research Quarterly*, 55(4), 601-623.

Miller, C. (2019). *Know my name: A memoir*. Viking.

Reed, A. (2019). *The nowhere girls*. Simon & Schuster.

Ryan, E. & Hurst, H. (2021). Bullying always seemed less complicated before I read: Developing adolescents' understandings of the complex social architecture of bullying through a YAL book club. *Research in the Teaching of English, 55*(4), 416-440.

Yang, K. (2020). *Parachutes*. Katherine Tegen Books.

Introduction

In an ideal world, a book like this would not be needed. Unfortunately, we live in reality, where harmful acts of sexual violence manifest as staggering statistics. According to the Centers for Disease Control and Prevention (CDC, 2022), sexual violence is pervasive, with "over half of all women experiencing sexual violence involving physical contact" at some point in their lives. Sexual violence can happen to anyone; in fact, 1 in 3 men have also experienced sexual violence of a physical nature (CDC, 2022). Most survivors report that their first sexual assault occurred before the age of 25 (CDC, 2022).

The National Sexual Violence Resource Center (NSVRC) notes that 1 in 5 women experience "completed or attempted rape during their lifetime," and a high number of female survivors know their attackers (NSVRC, 2022). While these numbers primarily address male and female statistics, it is crucial to recognize that individuals of all genders and ages can experience sexual violence. These statistics paint a grave picture of how many Americans, particularly young Americans, are impacted by sexual violence.

In this volume, we use the term 'rape culture' to refer to a societal environment that normalizes, trivializes, or even condones sexual violence and its perpetrators, while blaming victims for their own abuse. Rape culture encompasses a range of attitudes, beliefs, and behaviors that contribute to a culture where sexual violence is pervasive, and survivors are often disbelieved, stigmatized, or silenced. This culture may manifest in various forms, including victim-blaming, the objectification of bodies, the glamorization of sexual aggression in media, and the reinforcement of traditional gender roles. Ultimately, rape culture perpetuates a cycle of harm by maintaining harmful stereotypes, minimizing the impact of sexual violence, and undermining efforts to hold perpetrators accountable. Recognizing and challenging rape culture is essential in creating a society where all individuals are valued, respected, and free from the threat of sexual violence.

As co-editors of this volume, we feel it is important to articulate our positionalities, which encompass both our professional backgrounds and our personal experiences. We, Kate and Brittany, are both cisgender white women and literacy educators deeply immersed in the field of teacher preparation. Our experiences as teachers, coupled with our lived experiences within a rape culture, have profoundly shaped our understanding of and orientation to this work. These experiences have instilled in us a sense of urgency and commitment to addressing the pervasive impact of rape culture and advocating for all survivors' voices to be heard.

Fundamentally, we hold the belief that rape culture is not only real but also pervasive, permeating nearly all facets of society. It is our conviction that we bear a moral obligation to disrupt the silence surrounding rape culture and advocate for its eradication. Through our professional roles, we have witnessed firsthand the importance of addressing these issues with adolescents and young adults. We firmly believe that this demographic both desires and requires comprehensive education on topics related to sexual violence. We recognize the transformative potential of young adult literature and other youth texts in facilitating meaningful discussions and fostering critical thinking on this subject matter.

However, we must also acknowledge the limitations inherent in our positionalities. Our privileged identities inevitably shape our perspectives and influence the scope of our understanding. We are acutely aware that current representations of sexual violence often fail to adequately capture the diverse experiences of survivors, particularly those who hold multiple marginalized identities. Victims who fall outside of dominant narratives are frequently erased or overlooked. In our commitment to disrupting systems of power, we endeavor to confront and challenge our own biases, recognizing that our ongoing growth and self-reflection are integral to effecting meaningful change.

As we navigate the complexities of this work, we remain steadfast in our dedication to amplifying marginalized voices, advocating for social justice, and contributing to the collective effort to dismantle rape culture and create a safer, more inclusive world for all.

The following edited volume is composed of three distinctive parts of an overarching whole. Each chapter addresses a different facet of the discussion on rape culture and youth texts and their implications for teaching and learning. Some chapters contain specific teaching ideas and approaches, while others offer considerations from author reflection and text analysis and their potential to inform pedagogical choices in classrooms.

Part I: Making Space for Conversations about Rape Culture in Schools

Each chapter within this section provides teachers and teacher educators with thoughtful information, frameworks, and ideas for making space to hold difficult conversations around youth texts that address rape culture.

For example, we open this section with Molly C. Driessen's chapter, *Social Media as a Teachable Text: How Teachers Can Learn From and Use Social Media to Prepare for Discussions About Rape Culture*. Driessen looks to the world of social media to consider what educators can glean from survivor comments online and how these conversations can inform schooling-based practice.

Next, Gillian Mertens's chapter, *Sexual Assault in Young Adult Literature: Mirrors and Windows Into Experiences of Survivorship*, addresses how a survivorship lens can be used to create thoughtful and responsive spaces for students when reading novels that directly address sexual violence and rape culture.

Finally, Part I closes with, *The Sharp Edge of Silence: Using a Young Adult Novel to C.A.R.E. For Students*, written by Emily Pendergrass, Melanie Hundley, Michael Neel, and Kathryn Pendergrass. This chapter draws on a vignette as the impetus for considering how the C.A.R.E framework can create thoughtful classroom environments to hold difficult discussions around rape culture and youth texts.

Part II: Critical Analysis of Youth Texts

This section is composed of three chapters, each delving into one or more texts that address rape culture. Each chapter pulls forth powerful implications for classroom practice that directly relate to the author's analysis.

Part II opens with Elizabeth Marshall and Amber Moore's chapter, *"I want my entrance fee back": Institutional Betrayal in Young Adult Sexual Assault Narratives*, which addresses how fictional boarding schools can mirror how institutions can uphold rape culture and how students and teachers can address these systems of oppression.

Next, Shelby Boehm, Henry Cody Miller, and Lorelei Starkey analyze setting in fictional YAL as sociological sites that create insiders and outsiders in the aftermath of sexual violence, in their chapter entitled *Social, Communal, and Familial: Examining Isolation through Setting Analysis in Sexual Assault Young Adult Literature*.

Finally, Mark A. Lewis and Luke Rodesiler's chapter, *Male Youth-Athletes as Victims of Sexual Violence in Recommended Sports-Related Young Adult Literature*, analyses how the fictional experience of rape culture in sport-related settings can make space for discussions regarding challenging rape culture.

Part III: Critical Understandings, Teaching, and Application

The final section of this volume includes three chapters that make space for real world changes by challenging rape culture. This section focuses on practical applications and strategies for educators to confront and disrupt rape culture in their teaching practices.

The fist chapter in this section, *Disrupting Rape Myths and Objective Violence through Graphic Novels: A Critical Literacy Approach to Educating Emergent Bilingual*

Youth by Jie Park, provides researchers with conclusions from a study on bilingual students learning about rape culture.

The second chapter, by Brittany Adams, *"It shouldn't take you personally knowing a potential victim to start being a decent person": Exploring the Importance of Vulnerability in Critical Literacy Learning* directly considers notions of vulnerability and teaching about rape culture and what teachers of all grades and levels can learn from critally reflecting on their practice.

Finally, Cameron Greensmith, Adam Davies, and Jocelyn Sakal Froese, draw on the popular TV show, *Euphoria,* to consider what teachers can learn about rape culture in their chapter: *The Anti-Hero: Negotiating Rape Culture, Suicide Intensity, and Neoliberal Belonging.*

Closing Thoughts

As we delve into the important discussions presented within this volume, it is crucial to acknowledge a pervasive issue that persists not only within the realm of literature but also within the broader discourse surrounding rape culture and sexual violence education. Moreover, the dearth of diversity in the young adult literature (YAL) featured in this volume highlights a troubling trend within the literary landscape. Too often, narratives surrounding sexual violence are filtered through a limited lens, privileging certain identities and experiences while marginalizing others. This not only silences the voices of those who have been historically marginalized but also has the potential to perpetuate harmful myths and misconceptions about who is deemed worthy of empathy and support in discussions of rape culture. As editors, we believe that we need more inclusive stories in youth texts that highlight a multitude of experiences and identities.

It is an unfortunate truth that many voices dominating the conversation on rape culture and sexual violence education often reflect a narrow demographic scope, failing to encompass the diverse array of experiences and perspectives that exist within our society. This lack of representation perpetuates systemic inequalities and reinforces harmful stereotypes, ultimately hindering our ability to foster meaningful and inclusive dialogues on these critical issues. When we developed our call for this volume, it was our hope to capture a wide range of voices and perspectives to better inform the important work of teachers and teacher educators striving to address rape culture in their classrooms. While this volume contains many important chapters and perspectives, we as editors must address the lack of diversity in both the authors contributing to this collection and the representation within the YAL examined herein.

It is imperative that we recognize this inherent bias and actively work to dismantle it. As teachers and teacher educators, we must strive to center the experiences of those who have been historically overlooked or silenced in our classrooms. By doing so, we can ensure students have access to a more inclusive and representative body of literature that reflects the complex realities of sexual violence and its impact on individuals from all walks of life. Thus, this volume is not meant to represent everyone's stories. Instead, this text offers included authors' research, perspectives, and suggestions for practice. These chapters are important facets of ongoing discussions in the field, and we hope that these chapters further the work of confronting issues of sexual violence and rape culture in commonplace youth texts.

In acknowledging these challenges, we must also recognize the power and potential of literature to effect change. By engaging critically with the texts presented in this volume, we have an opportunity to challenge existing narratives, disrupt harmful stereotypes, and cultivate empathy and understanding for students. Let us embrace this opportunity to create a more equitable and just society for all.

References

Center for Disease Control and Prevention (CDC). (2022). *Fast facts: Preventing sexual violence.* https://www.cdc.gov/violenceprevention/sexualviolence/fastfact.html

I. Making Space for Conversations about Rape Culture in Schools

Social Media as a Teachable Text: How Teachers Can Learn From and Use Social Media to Prepare for Discussions About Rape Culture

Molly C. Driessen, Providence College

Given the high prevalence of sexual violence among youth, specifically individuals ages 13-18 (CDC, 2021), researchers, practitioners, and educators must creatively and critically identify and explore ways to prevent, educate, and advocate to end sexual violence, including within the classroom. Teachers and teacher educators have begun to consider how social media may be used as a tool to engage with their students and increase their own awareness and education about a variety of topics and social issues, including those related to sexual education, activism, and disclosures (Dennen et al., 2020; Duggan, 2023). As researchers have demonstrated, youth user engagement with social media continues to increase (Marciano et al., 2022). Students have actively sought out online spaces to share their stories of sexual violence, find solidarity, learn from others about their experiences, and seek help, all under the protection of privacy and anonymity (Bogen et al., 2021). However, more research is needed to better understand how youth engage with social media, the stories they share, and how teachers may identify strategies from these stories to better support their students (Duggan, 2023). To that end, this chapter explores one profile on the social media platform of Instagram to explore how users engage with social media to share their stories of sexual violence.

Defining and Describing the Impact of Rape Culture

Sexual violence can be defined as any attempted or completed sexual contact without consent (Smith et al., 2018). Although statistics vary, approximately 1 in 3 women and nearly 1 in 6 men have experienced some type of sexual violence during their lifetime (Smith et al., 2018). Sexual violence is prevalent among youth, including 41% of female-identifying survivors having reported being raped before the age of 18 (Smith et al., 2018). A 2021 survey found that approximately 20% of surveyed female-identifying students in grades 9-12 had experienced sexual violence during the past year (CDC, 2021). Sexual violence impacts all demographics, but research continue to demonstrate higher prevalence rates for youth who may identify as lesbian, gay, bisexual, questioning, or another non-heterosexual identity (LGBTQ+) (CDC, 2021). Further, the majority of survivors do not formally report their assault, indicating that prevalence rates are likely higher than what is known across all genders (Banvard-Fox et al., 2022; Smith et al., 2018). Reasons for not reporting can include fear of not being believed, fear that what happened does not warrant a crime or report, and other rape culture myths related to feelings of self-blame, guilt, and shame (Fisher et al., 2003; Orchowski et al., 2022).

Survivors of sexual violence may experience a variety of mental health concerns, including depression, anxiety, suicidal ideation, substance use, and post-traumatic stress disorder (Exner-Cortens et al., 2013; Jouriles et al., 2017). Other public health concerns include teen pregnancy, infections, and physical health concerns (Banvard-Fox et al., 2022; Bright et al., 2016). Youth, along with their guardians, also are likely to have to navigate various legal issues, including age of consent, age of statutory rape, child welfare systems, and maximum age difference permissible for legal sexual activity among minors, all of which vary across states (Banvard-Fox et al., 2022). Similar to the low rates of formal reporting, researchers have found low rates of help-seeking among youth survivors of sexual violence (Lachman et al., 2019). In a study of dating youth in the U.S., 59% reported having experienced some type of dating abuse victimization (Lachman et al., 2019). Lachman and colleagues (2019) found that only 9% of victims reported seeking help, with female-identifying victims being more likely to seek help than male victims, and that 17% of youth sought help from school counselors and 13% from teachers.

In addition to the myriad outcomes that a survivor may navigate following an assault, a rape culture also significantly shapes sexual violence. Rape culture can be described as beliefs, values, and attitudes that reinforce sexual violence as normal and a result of the survivor's behavior, demeanor, appearance, use of substances, among other considerations (Herman, 1984; Zaleski et al., 2016). These beliefs and practices permeate society and have negative consequences for survivors seeking help, reporting, and healing through their trauma (Zaleski et al., 2016)

Teaching about Rape Culture

Researchers have identified various aspects for educators to consider when teaching about sensitive topics, including ones that may be controversial or stigmatized, including sexual education and violence (Clonan-Roy et al., 2021; Duggan, 2023). Some researchers, for example, have examined the negative consequences and harm of current sexual health education programs within the U.S., including concerns that current textbooks and curricula can negatively impact already harmful rape culture myths (Clonan-Roy et al., 2021; Klement et al., 2022). Some curricula and textbooks have been found to highlight strategies that reinforce messages of victim-blaming, particular for female-identifying students, including that abstinence should be the primary safety strategy, that the lack of abstinence increases risk of rape, and other personal strategies that place the sole responsibility on would-be victims (Clonan-Roy et al., 2021).

Researchers have identified other challenges with discussing sexual violence in schools, including teachers' discomfort or conflicting values and beliefs (Klement et al., 2022). Even well-meaning teachers may inadvertently express or perform beliefs or values that reinforce rape myths and decrease the likelihood of students breaking their silence, asking for help, or reporting (Klement et al., 2022). Teachers must also manage reactions to depictions or discussions of sexual violence from both students and parents, including ones that are likely to be emotionally intense and potentially challenging within certain moral or political territories (Duggan, 2023). These challenges have elicited calls from many scholars (Duggan, 2023; Miller et al., 2023) to study and identify potential strategies and supports for addressing this critical topic within the classroom.

The Role of Social Media Among Youth

According to the Pew Research Center (2022), 95% of teenagers engage with YouTube, followed by TikTok at 67%, and Instagram and Snapchat, which is reportedly used by 1 in 6 youth. Like the rest of the world, adolescents increased their engagement of digital devices and social media during the COVID-19 pandemic (Marciano et al., 2022). Researchers, particularly exploring the role of the pandemic, have identified both potentially positive (e.g., social connection) and negative (e.g., increase mental health concerns) aspects to social media use (Marciano et al., 2022; Ramsey et al., 2023; Zhang et al., 2021).

As previously noted, the majority of survivors do not formally report their experiences of sexual violence. However, many individuals disclose their experiences to an informal person, such as friends or family (Fisher et al., 2003). The responses that survivors receive are critical to their healing and, although some individuals may receive positive responses, many do not (Lorenz et al., 2018). As a result, individuals are increasingly turning to social media as a platform to disclose their experiences (Bogen et al., 2021).

The increasing use of social media by youth, coupled with concerns about both potentially positive and negative impacts, researchers must continue to study the multifacetedness and immediate, daily integral presence of social media in youths' lives (Marciano et al., 2022; Ramsey et al., 2013; Zhang et al., 2021). I argue that teachers, in particular, and school systems, as a whole, have an opportunity and responsibility to think about how to best leverage social media's potential, including opportunities to educate and raise awareness about potentially controversial and stigmatized topics, like sexual violence, and to address concerns of social isolation and mental health, both of which survivors of sexual violence are likely to experience in navigating post-assault life (Jouriles et al., 2017).

Researchers have studied social media as it relates to education and use among youth since its inception, including the use of social media as a teaching and learning tool (Dennen et al., 2020). Teachers have explored how to best use social media as a tool to educate students inside and outside the classroom, especially given the high usage and content that youth may engage with online (Chugh & Ruhi, 2018; Dennen et al., 2020). As such, social media may be considered a unique teachable text, offering content, strategies, and lessons learned for educators looking to bring this content area into the classroom. Although not a formal, traditional source of knowledge like textbooks or other toolkits often used in K-12 settings, social media still provides text and content in new, emerging, and nuanced ways to think through as teachable content.

In their review of recent research studies exploring social media as it relates to education, Dennen et al. (2020) found that overall research in this area continues to grow and that key themes found in the data included the overall use of social media as a teaching and learning tool, themes around digital literacy, digital citizenship, social relationships, identity development and expression, effects of use, and communication, among others. Furthermore, not only were educators identifying and exploring ways to use social media within and outside of the classroom but so were parents, students, staff, and other school community members. This area of scholarship continues to grow in expanding strategies for educators and teachers to use and incorporate social media, and general awareness of how youth are engaging with it.

Scholars also have noted even the potential ways that social media can be leveraged for topics that some educators may feel censored in or spaces where certain topics, like sexual violence, may not be so explicitly discussed (Dennen et al., 2020; Duggan, 2023). Given the themes of silence, stigma, and rape myths surrounding sexual violence that are prevalent in society, educators can be proactive in their use of social media to potentially prevent and/or minimize the spread of misinformation and increase awareness of not only accurate information but also information that is survivor centered (Duggan, 2023). Other scholars have also noted the accessibility of social media, including anonymity and privacy, even arguing that some spaces on social media reflect more diverse, intersectional, and democratic spaces for students and individuals with varying experiences of trauma, power, privilege, and oppression to voice concerns, engage in solidarity, and find a sense of community (Duggan, 2023; Mendes et al., 2019).

Researchers continue to study the varying social reactions that survivors may receive when disclosing in online spaces, the potential mental health impacts (both negative and positive) of these disclosures, and even survivors who choose not to disclose but engage in online survivor spaces and may be impacted in a variety of ways through being exposed to content that can be incredibly traumatizing (Alaggia & Wang, 2020; Bogen et al., 2021; Gorissen et al., 2023; PettyJohn et al., 2022). Based on this collective research, further clinical recommendations must be developed for mental health practitioners working with survivors of sexual violence who may find engaging with social media to be very healing but also potentially traumatizing (PettyJohn et al., 2022).

In other words, social media is not an inherently safe, healing, or survivor-centered space to be in, and educators, parents, and other caregivers need to not only recognize this but also learn strategies to support any young person operating in these spaces. For further reading on potential recommendations and strategies specifically for parents navigating digital spaces in general, I highly recommend Dr. Devorah Heitner's research. In her book, *Growing Up in Public: Coming of Age in a Digital World* (Heitner, 2023) provides numerous strategies, debunks various myths and stereotypes, and validates fears and concerns primarily for a parent audience looking to support their young person in navigating these terrains. Nonetheless, more research, including qualitative studies, is needed to better understand and develop safe and trauma-informed strategies within and outside the classroom in the use of social media (Dennen & Rutledge, 2018; Dennen et al., 2020).

Brief Description of the Research Study

The examples from social media that will be discussed in this chapter came from a research study that explored the phenomenon of youth engagement with social media, specifically Instagram, as a platform to disclose experiences of sexual violence. The majority of posts from the original profile used were specific to sexual violence experiences on college campuses. However, the study used for this chapter only focused on the sample that indicated sexual violence explicit to youth experiences prior to attending college. Data on stories specific to campus sexual violence experiences were reported on in a different study (Driessen, under review).

This chapter explores how social media could be used as a multimodal text and tool, specifically by educators, to teach youth about topics related to sexual violence and rape culture. Through a qualitative research design using phenomenology (Vagle, 2014; Van Manen, 2014) and thematic analysis (Braun & Clarke, 2006), this study was guided by the following questions: What can teachers and educators learn from disclosures on social media of youth experiences of sexual violence? How can social media be a teachable text to address rape culture and myths within and outside of the classroom?

It is important to note this study adhered to ethical considerations outlined by previous researchers when engaging with social media narratives (Bruckman, 2002; Eysenbach & Till, 2001). For example, to further protect any potential user information, all identifying information, including specific information about the user's institution, was redacted. The profile itself already kept all users' information confidential and posts anonymous. Given the anonymous nature of the posts, demographic information about the user could not be inferred.

While all of the data examined in this study is publicly available, this research was undertaken with great ethical concern. Though I submitted a proposal for this project to my institution's internal review board, they determined that this study was considered exempt.

Positionality

As a social work educator-scholar-practitioner, I have worked at the intersections of sexual violence work across micro, mezzo, and macro systems. Social workers are interested in the person and environment approach, systems-based thinking, and have explicit values and ethics rooted in social justice and social change (National Association of Social Workers (NASW), 2021). Although I engage extensively in research around related topics of gender-based violence, trauma, and resilience, I also engage with these topics in my clinical practice and in the classroom, most recently with undergraduate students. I am a white, heterosexual cisgender female, who can operate within systems, like academia, with immense power and privilege.

However, I also identify as a victim-survivor of sexual violence, and these experiences have significantly shaped me personally and professionally. Although it is still common to receive fear-based responses upon this disclosure, my experience and personal commitment to this work is not unique. I join many scholars, activists, and practitioners who are involved in this work given their own personal stories, and researchers have continued to identify the unique and strengths-based perspectives that these can bring to this work (Petillo & Hlavka, 2022). As a scholar I am deeply intentional about alignment with my methodologies and analysis, as well as being explicitly aware of what frames my seeing and naming it. For example, phenomenology is a qualitative method that provides space for researchers to critically reflect, name, and integrate their intersecting identities and experiences and how these may frame and impact the study (Vagle, 2014; Van Manen, 2014).

Key Themes and Examples To Consider

In this section, five key themes are presented to describe how users engaged with social media to share their lived experiences of sexual violence. These themes included users' descriptions of **someone they trusted**, fear of not being believed, experiences of shame, reflections on surviving, and describing what change looks like. The first theme, **someone they trusted**, included users describing how the sexual violence occurred with a friend, romantic partner, family member, or in environments where a sense of trust had been established. In **fear of not being believed**, users shared about reporting processes, confronting rumors, and not knowing what to do. The third theme included **shame** that users felt towards their self and from others, particularly in relation to rape culture and myths, descriptions of feeling "dirty", and feelings of self-blame and guilt. The fourth theme, **surviving**, encompassed reflections of surviving post-assault, including mental health, getting help, finding spaces to be heard, and reminding others that they are not alone. In the last theme, **describing what change looks like**, users discussed consent and bodily autonomy, accountability, the role of education, finding support, and learning about healthy relationships.

Someone They Trusted

Users frequently described their perpetrator as someone they had established trust with, whether general familiarity, a friend, family member, or a friend of a friend. In other words, for many users, they had no reason to doubt this individual. One person described, "I was raped by a classmate and a 'friend' of over 5 years." Another shared, "I was sexually assaulted by my ex-boyfriend in my own home." Some users also reflected on the level of coercion or manipulation they could now name looking back, due to having trusted the person. A person describing their perpetrator said, "My first boyfriend made me think that love was manipulation and guilt." Another summarized, "I thought it was all normal, and then I realized it wasn't, and I really struggled to accept it as it was, and still do to this day, years later." Users described their excitement about either being in new relationships, feeling the attention of someone they looked up to, or the social dynamics of trying to make new friends or be invited to a party. In describing some of these social contexts of where trust was violated, an individual shared, "I trusted him, and I was also eager to make a new friend." A second one shared, "I was sexually abused/assaulted by a close friend, a person I never thought would do anything like that." Posters shared stories of trust violated with a neighbor, step-brother, friend, cousin, grandpa, teacher, peers, older classmates, graduates of their school, a doctor, and a friend's family member.

Fear of Not Being Believed

Potentially impacted by the degree of trust that they had formed with their perpetrator, and being aware of how others may then view their story, users shared their fear of not being believed. Within this fear of not being believed, users were acutely aware of the social dynamics surrounding their story, including the impacts of not formally reporting due to their fear of not being believed. Yet, in not reporting, some individuals described almost a vicious cycle of knowing that no one may possibly believe them. A user said, "I didn't report him or ask for help because it was too late out of fear of looking weak." Another said, "I didn't take it to court because I knew I had no evidence and would lose." A person shared, "I'm scared to tell a lot of people." Within the context of fearing not being believed, users also described how the other individual involved was still known and trusted by their community, even within leadership roles, and how challenging it was to witness these dynamics and the impact on their story. A user shared,

> It became unbearable watching everyone treat him like a god (it was a very small school and he was very charismatic and popular . . . I slowly started to tell more people . . . I expected support and some sort of justice from my schoolmates but instead I was met with judgment. . . everyone rushed to comfort HIM and completely ignored me. . . saying that I must be lying if I waited so long to say anything and didn't report it. I lost all of my friends because I spoke out.

Another wrote, "He said if I tried to say anything I had no proof, so no one would believe me." A person shared, "I felt like I couldn't come forward with my story . . . he was our class President and well-liked by everyone." For users who did share their story with others or formerly report, many described ongoing aspects of not being believed by those in power and leadership. A user wrote, "I reported this to the principal's office in graphic detail, they did nothing, they said there was no evidence, they told him to just give me space." Some individuals also described how the impact of these social dynamics and fear of not being believed, and often explicit moments of peers and those in power not believing their story, made them question their story, sense of self, and if what had happened was "really" a sexual assault. A user shared the ongoing impact of not being believed as, "I still struggle with thinking that my rape wasn't actually rape." Another shared, "I decided that I needed to report the incident to my school. When I did, they told me that they didn't think that what happened was assault at all."

Shame

Users described shame in several ways. First, some individuals described the shame that they felt toward themselves and from others, and how this shame impacted decisions to share their story. A user said, "I was too ashamed to admit that I was raped." Another said, "My biggest regret is feeling ashamed." A person wrote, "I thought I would share because I am so tired of holding this shame inside of me and I think if I bottle it up any longer I will go crazy." Many users also shared experiences of being called a "slut", "slut-shamed", or other derogatory stories that they heard others saying about their "hook-up". A person wrote, "She [a friend] texted me calling me a slut." Another said, "She [a friend] said that it [the assault] happened because I was slutty." Users reflected on how these comments negatively contributed to their already held sense of feeling "dirty", a feeling that some almost felt immediately after their assault. One person wrote, "I showered for four hours. I stayed in the shower long after we had run out of hot water, literally trying to scrub off every inch of skin that he had touched." Another shared, "My skin feels unclean." A user reflected, "Every day I went home feeling dirty and disgusted with myself." Within this theme of shame, users described how much these negative comments and blaming from others increased their own self-blame and shame. Individuals connected these feelings related to shame to broader societal rape myths and culture, particularly describing feelings of self-blame and guilt. A person said, "I never said a thing due to the fact that I thought I was going to be blamed for what he was doing." Users frequently wrote similar posts to describe these feelings of self-blame, such as, "For years I blamed myself", "I felt so stupid and blamed myself for so long", "I was victim-blamed", "I have blamed myself for years", and, "I thought I had done something wrong to deserve it." Finally, one person wrote, "You learn that for whatever reason shame and blame are the only languages in this world we are allowed to speak."

Surviving

Users shared many different stories of what surviving looked liked for them, which for some included being able to use this social media space to share their story anonymously for the first time. A person said, "I know this is long lol sorry I kinda just needed to let it out! Thanks for providing a safe space for us to be heard." A user also wrote,

> Even if you don't post this, I just wanted to thank you so much for giving survivors the opportunity to tell their story. This is the first time I've told mine and it feels so liberating. I don't know if I would ever tell my story publicly, but I believe this is my first step towards healing.

Another wrote, "It's still hard now to deal with, but here's my story." Finally, one wrote, "I never thought I would share publicly, but given this forum and a chance to shed light on intoxication and assault, I will leave this here." Within the theme of surviving, users described their mental health and well-being, including immediately following the assault through their present day. A person wrote, "I was diagnosed with PTSD [post-traumatic stress disorder] after, and the validation I felt from that diagnosis was insurmountable." For some users, it continued to be a journey to process their experience. A user shared, "I don't even know how to explain how it affected me. It's not something I'm really able to process even now." Other individuals described experiences of anxiety, negative body image, self-esteem, eating disorders, dissociation, depression, and suicidality, among others. Users also shared experiences with disclosure, when they asked for and actively sought out help. One person wrote, "I'm so grateful to have friends and family that have shown me what real love is." A user shared, "Luckily my parents were supportive and got me the help I needed." Finally, individuals described the importance of moments when they felt heard and were less alone, and using these moments to encourage others that they are also not alone. In feeling heard and less alone, users felt supported in their post-assault survival journey. One person wrote, "Reading these stories has encouraged me to write and remember that no one is ever alone." Similarly, a user said, "I guess at the end of the day, what I want to say is that I hope no one ever has to feel alone." Likewise, a poster reflected, "I just want other girls to know that they are not alone." Another said, "Thank you to all the people who have come out and given me the strength to come out too." Finally, one user wrote, "I'm really grateful for a community like this . . . only love, support, and some really good listeners. So, to those who did listen to my story, thank you."

Change Looks Like

In continuing to build upon the theme of surviving, users shared in their posts what they believe change could look like. For some individuals, they described this theme in providing spaces like this social media account for stories to be shared. One user summarized, "Providing a safe space for us to be heard." Another said, "I hope that through these stories being shared it can eventually change because no one deserves to be treated like that." Similarly, a user wrote, "Help us get our voices heard!" Other individuals focused on education and awareness, including around consent, bodily autonomy, sexuality, and what healthy relationships should look like. A person posted,

> Children need to be taught about consent and boundaries and respecting others and having autonomy over their own body from the moment they can understand words, and parents and teachers need to have ongoing conversations with them or else this horrible behavior will only continue.

A user encouraged others to, "Please look out for the warning signs." Likewise, a user wrote, "I am vocal about consent and advocating for those who have similar stories." Finally, individuals called for more accountability when reports are made and how increased accountability would require societal shifts in victim-blaming and rape myths. A person said, "[sexual violence] should not be considered normal in relationships or in any scenario. We normalize sexual abuse and harassment too readily and it's NOT OKAY." Another wrote, "People need to hold others more accountable for sexualizing children." Some users reflected on how a lack of accountability creates further opportunity for permissibility of abusive behavior. For example, a person commented, "I fear for all of the women he's probably done the same to, and he doesn't deserve to be where he is today."

Discussion and Recommendations

These key themes and examples from this specific social media profile will be discussed in relation to each other, previous research, and how youth educators can use social media as a teachable and trauma-informed text for students, fellow educators, administrators, and families. Strategies, including from what users shared about their experiences, will be discussed as potential resources for teachers and entire school communities to use within and outside their classrooms to debunk rape myths, broaden student and educators' understandings of sexual violence, and think more critically about cultural change across micro, mezzo, and macro levels within educational systems.

The themes from this study included users identifying that the perpetrator was someone they trusted, their fear of not being believed, feelings of shame, the hard process and journey of surviving following their assault, and describing what change could look like. Within the first theme, users described how the person who sexually assaulted them was a person with whom trust had already been established to some degree. These trusted individuals were peers, authority or leader figures, and family, friends, or romantic partners. Furthermore, not only were these individuals with whom the person had trusted, but the users were acutely aware of how others had trusted and perceived them as well.

Users described the challenges of navigating the resulting social and power dynamics of understanding how their perpetrator was also perceived by others in a respectful, positive manner, and the challenging impact of being believed because of this dynamic. Users shared how extensively they felt this fear of not being believed, a fear, which for many, was frequently confirmed by their peers, authority figures, and even family members when they did share their story or report. The fear of not being believed also impacted their emotional well-being and mental health, with posters sharing how when others questioned their experience, they too began to doubt or question their experience, leading to feelings of guilt, victim-blaming, and shame.

Users described how these feelings of intense shame impacted their emotional and mental well-being and that they were aware of how societal rape myths influenced not only their individual experience but also how others perceived of their experience. Considering this, posters shared varying aspects of what surviving looked like, including challenges of mental health, feelings of loneliness, isolation, or loss of friend groups and social dynamics. Within the theme of surviving, however, users identified how supportive some relationships were, including parents, for providing positive and affirming responses to their stories and making them feel less alone. Users also frequently recognized how critical this social media platform was in feeling less alone and the resulting motivation of wanting to make others feel less alone, including the desire to give hope for other victim-survivors to survive.

Besides descriptions of surviving, users shared what change could look like to prevent sexual violence and provide stronger and more positive responses to support victim-survivors. Users identified the importance of being believed, heard, and listened to, earlier education about consent, bodily autonomy, and warning signs within school, accountability for when reports are made, and not normalizing sexual violence or predatory behaviors within relationships, including awareness specific to dating violence. To begin to address some of the recommendations and needs described by the users, teachers and teacher educators may consider several strategies, discussed below, found within extant scholarship (CDC, 2021; Dennen et al., 2020; Duggan, 2023).

Teacher Training and Professional Development

First, school systems can develop and offer professional development workshops focused both on the use of social media (Dennen et al., 2020; Duggan, 2023) as a learning tool and on content specific to sexual violence, including debunking rape myths, decreasing stigma, awareness on prevalence rates, as well as information on reporting, policies, and resources. Social media, coupled with intentional professional development training that takes up intersectional and culturally informed approaches, can also assist teachers in learning how to be aware of their own biases, stereotypes, and beliefs that may contribute to rape myths and other harmful opinions that can be detrimental to supporting victim-survivors.

Student Survivor Voices as Case Studies

Alongside learning more about youth sexual violence, teachers can begin to review these stories on social media to learn directly from youth experiences, their recommendations, and what they need. Teachers will inevitably have their own personal values and emotional responses that they will need to manage when discussing, responding to, and teaching this and related content. Within professional development workshops and creating other sexual violence working groups in schools, teachers can provide support to one another in discussing this material, sharing reactions, discussing resources and content, and reaching out to local experts and resources for how to best address and respond to student voices and needs. In creating spaces for increasing education, awareness, and collaboration, school systems can become more equitable spaces (CDC, 2021).

Access to Mental Health Services, Potential Resources, and Review of Policies

Other recommendations include using social media to inform increasing access to mental health services, including services that explicitly focus on survivor experiences, increasing awareness and access to reporting, and holding individuals, especially those who are in leadership and positions of power within school systems, accountable for their behavior. Teachers are uniquely positioned to educate not only themselves but also their students about these services, resources, and policies, particularly around reporting, confidentiality, and options. In turn, teachers can take what they learn in the classroom from students and social media back to school leadership to help strengthen these systems to be survivor-centered.

Bolstering Social Connection and Support

Scholars also have recommended building upon critical protective factors, particularly around social connectedness (CDC, 2021; Murthy, 2023). Students who identify as female, as a student of color, and as LGBTQ+ are least likely to experience social connectedness within school systems (CDC, 2021), yet have high prevalence rates of sexual violence when compared to their other peers (Banvard-Fox et al., 2022). Researchers already have shared concerns related to feelings of isolation and loneliness among youth, increasingly in recent years (Murthy, 2023). Consequently, teachers and entire school communities can integrate social media to build upon these protective factors to foster relationships and social connection, even from the starting point of recognizing that students may turn to social media as a space to connect given lack of connection within in-person environments.

Trauma and Culturally Informed Teaching

Furthermore, as part of these collaborations, teachers, working alongside other experts and service providers in their local area, can consider how to appropriately identify specific stories to share within the classroom to bring awareness and education to all students, including giving the opportunity for students to discuss their own biases, beliefs, and stereotypes. However, these spaces need to be intentionally designed in trauma-informed (SAMHSA, 2014) and culturally-informed ways to mitigate potential harm, especially for students who may have experienced sexual violence or related trauma. In implementing these strategies and becoming more aware of the impact and prevalence of sexual violence within schools, educational communities can work towards become more trauma-informed systems.

Although definitions vary, individual trauma results from an event(s) experienced by an individual as physically or emotionally harmful or life threatening and that has lasting adverse effects on the individual's functioning and well-being (SAMHSA, 2014). SAMHSA (2014) has outlined six principles to consider when implementing a trauma-informed approach. These key principles include addressing safety, trustworthiness and transparency, peer support, collaboration and mutuality, empowerment, voice, and choice, and cultural, historical, and gender issues (SAMHSA, 2014). A trauma-informed teaching approach acknowledges and assumes that students have been affected by trauma and that, in being able to recognize trauma symptoms, educators and school systems can respond more appropriately by integrating this knowledge into policies, practices, and, ultimately, resist retraumatization (Harris & Fallot, 2001; Hitchcock et al., 2021; SAMHSA, 2014).

Conclusion

School systems have a responsibility and unique opportunity to consider how to use and integrate social media as a learning tool in a myriad of ways. Given the ongoing reports of mental health, trauma, and other challenges that youth continue to navigate, teachers and teacher educators need to consider all potential tools to strengthen response efforts critically and creatively. Researchers continue to report that most survivors do not formally report their assault (Banvard-Fox et al., 2022) and that those who do are often faced with victim-blaming, shame, and other rape culture beliefs, opinions, and attitudes (Fisher et al., 2003; Orchowski et al., 2022). Social media may be one potential resource for teachers and all school community members to listen to survivors and learn directly from them about their experiences and recommendations for change. Educators can directly see what students are sharing and how this information can be used to inform classroom content and conversations, as well as inform school policies, procedures, and resources. Furthermore, as previously noted, the recommendations from this study directly provided from users have the potential to create stronger, healthier, and more trauma-informed and equitable school systems for all stakeholders, including teachers, staff, administrators, students, families, and surrounding communities.

References

Alaggia, R., & Wang, S. (2020). "I never told anyone until the #metoo movement": What can we learn from sexual abuse and sexual assault disclosures made through social media?. *Child Abuse & Neglect, 103*, 1-10.

Banvard-Fox, C., Linger, M., Paulson, D. J., Cottrell, L., & Davidov, D. M. (2022). Sexual assault in adolescents. *Primary Care, 47*(2), 331-349.

Bogen, K. W., Orchowski, L. M., & Ullman, S. E. (2021). Online disclosures of sexual victimization and social reactions: What do we know?. *Women & Therapy, 44*(3-4), 358-373.

Braun, V., & Clarke, V. (2006). Using thematic analysis in psychology. *Qualitative Research in Psychology, 3*(2), 77-101.

Bright, M. A., Knapp, C., Hinojosa, M. S., Alford, S., & Bonner, B. (2016). The comorbidity of physical, mental, and developmental conditions associated with childhood adversity: A population based study. *Maternal Child Health Journal, 20*, 843-853.

Bruckman, A. (2002). *Ethical guidelines for research online*. https://faculty.cc.gatech.edu/~asb/ethics/

Centers for Disease Control and Prevention (CDC). (2021). *Youth risk behavior survey: Data summary and trends report*. https://www.cdc.gov/healthyyouth/data/yrbs/yrbs_data_summary_and_trends.htm

Chugh, R., & Ruhi, U. (2018). Social media in higher education: A literature review of Facebook. *Education Information Technology, 23*, 605-616.

Clonan-Roy, K., Goncy, E. A., Naser, S. C., Fuller, K. A., DeBoard, A., Williams, A., & Hall, A. (2021). Preserving abstinence and preventing rape: How sex education textbooks contribute to rape culture. *Archives of Sexual Behavior, 50*, 231-245.

Dennen, V. P., & Rutledge, S. A. (2018). The embedded lesson approach to social media research: Researching online phenomena in an authentic offline setting. *TechTrends, 62*, 483-491.

Dennen, V. P., Choi, H., & Word, K. (2020). Social media, teenagers, and the school context: A scoping review of research in education and related fields. *Education Tech Research Dev, 68*, 1635-1658.

Duggan, J. (2023). Using TikTok to teach about abortion: Combating stigma and miseducation in the U.S. and beyond. *Sex Education, 23*(1), 81-95.

Duong, V., Pham, P., Bose, R., & Luo, J. (2020). #MeToo on campus: Studying college sexual assault at scale using data reported on social media. *ArXiv, Social and Information Networks*.

Eysenbach, G., & Till, J. E. (2001). Ethical issues in qualitative research on internet communities. *BMJ, 323*, 1103-1105.

Exner-Cortens, D., Eckenrode, J., & Rothman, E. (2013). Longitudinal associations between teen dating violence victimization and adverse health outcomes. *Pediatrics, 131*, 71-8.

Fisher, B., Daigle, L., Cullen, F., & Turner, M. (2003). Reporting sexual victimization to the police and others. *Criminal Justice and Behavior, 30*(1), 6-38.

Gorissen, M., van den Berg, C., Bijleveld, C., Ruiter, S., & Berenblum, T. (2021). Online disclosure of sexual victimization: A systematic review. *Trauma, Violence, Abuse*. 1-16.

Harris, M., & Fallot, R. D. (Eds.). (2001). *Using trauma theory to design service systems*. Jossey-Bass.

Heitner, D. (2023). *Growing up in public: Coming of age in a digital world*. Penguin Random House LLC.

Herman, D. (1984). The rape culture. In J. Freeman (Ed.), *Women: A feminist perspective*. Mountain View Press.

Hitchcock, L. I., Creswell Baez, J., Sage, M., Marquar, M., Lewis, K., & Smyth, N. J. (2021). Social work educators' opportunities during COVID-19: A roadmap for trauma-informed teaching during crisis. *Journal of Social Work Education, 57*, 82-98.

Jouriles, E. N., Choi, H. J., Rancher, C., & Temple, J. R. (2017). Teen dating violence victimization, trauma symptoms, and revictimization in early adulthood. *Journal of Adolescent Health, 61*, 115-119.

Klement, K. R., Sagarin, B. J., & Skowronski, J. J. (2022). The one ring model: Rape culture beliefs are linked to purity culture beliefs. *Sexuality & Culture, 26*, 2070-2106.

Lachman, P., Zweig, J., Dank, M., & Yahner, J. (2019). Patterns of help-seeking behavior among victims of teen dating violence and abuse: Variations among boys and girls. *Journal of School Health, 89*, 791-799.

Lorenz, K., Ullman, S. E., Kirkner, A., Mandala, R., Vasquez, A. L., & Sigurvinsdottir, R. (2018). Social reactions to sexual assault disclosure: A qualitative study of informal support dyads. *Violence Against Women, 24*(12), 1497-1520.

Marciano, L., Ostroumova, M., Schulz, P. J., & Camerini, A. (2022). Digital media use and adolescents' mental health during the Covid-19 pandemic: A systematic review and meta-analysis. *Frontiers in Public Health, 9*, 1-28.

Mendes, K., J. Ringrose, and J. Keller. (2019). *Digital feminist activism: Girls and women fight back against rape culture*. Oxford University Press.

Miller, H. C., Boehm, S., Colantonio-Yurko, K., Adams, B. & Mertens, G. (2023). Naming and challenging rape culture in English curriculum: A framework for teaching canonical texts with contemporary adaptations. *Changing English: Studies in Culture and Education, 2*(30), 117-129.

Murthy, V. H. (2023). *Our epidemic of loneliness and isolation: The U.S. Surgeon General's advisory on the healing effects of social connection and community.* https://www.hhs.gov/about/news/2023/05/03/new-surgeon-general-advisory-raises-alarm-about-devastating-impact-epidemic-loneliness-isolation-united-states.html#:~:text=Vivek%20Murthy%20released%20a%20new,experiencing%20measurable%20levels%20of%20loneliness.

National Association of Social Workers. (2021). *Code of ethics.* https://www.socialworkers.org/About/Ethics/Code-of-Ethics/Code-of-Ethics-English

Orchowski, L. M., Grocott, L., Bogen, K. W., et al. (2022). Barriers to reporting sexual violence: A qualitative analysis of #WhyIDidn'tReport. *Violence Against Women, 28*(4), 3530-3553.

Petillo, A. D. J., & Hlavka, H. R. (Eds.). (2022). *Researching gender-based violence: Embodied and intersectional approaches.* New York University Press.

PettyJohn, M. E., Anderson, G., & McCauley, H. L. (2022). Exploring survivor experiences on social media in the #MeToo era: Clinical recommendations for addressing impacts on mental health and relationships. *Journal of Interpersonal Violence, 37*(21-22), NP20677-NP20700.

Pew Research Center. (2022). *Teens, social media and technology.* [Report]. https://www.pewresearch.org/internet/2022/08/10/teens-social-media-and-technology-2022/

Ramsey, N., Obeidallah, M., & Abraham, A. (2023). Impact of Covid-19 on adolescent health and use of social media. *Journal of Curr Opin Pediatr, 35*(3), 362-367.

Substance Abuse and Mental Health Services Administration (SAMHSA). (2014). *SAMHSA's concept of trauma and guidance for a trauma-informed approach.* https://store/samhsa.gov/system/files/sma14-4884.pdf

Smith, S. G., . . . Chen, J. (2018). *The national intimate partner and sexual violence survey (NISVS): 2015 data brief-updated release.* National Center for Injury Prevention and Control. Centers for Disease Control and Prevention. https://www.cdc.gov/violenceprevention/pdf/2015data-bricf508.pdf

Vagle, M. (2014). *Crafting phenomenlogical research.* Left Coast Press.

Van Manen, M. (2014). *Phenomenology of practice: Meaning-giving methods in phenomenological research and writing.* Left Coast Press.

Zaleski, K. L., Gundersen, K. K., Baes, J., Estupinian, E., & Vergara, A. (2016). Exploring rape culture in social media forums. *Computers in Human Behavior, 63*, 922-927.

Zhang, S., Liu, M., Li, Y., & Chung, J. E. (2021). Teens' social media engagement during the Covid-19 pandemic: A time series examination of posting and emotion on reddit. *International Journal of Environmental Research and Public Health, 18*, 1-17.

Sexual Assault in Young Adult Literature: Mirrors and Windows Into Experiences of Survivorship

Gillian E. Mertens, SUNY Cortland

I was sexually assaulted in the early fall of my sophomore year of high school. Like many teen girls (NSVRC, 2018), this experience involved a peer acquaintance who I had regular contact with over the following years. The details of the assault are relatively irrelevant, except for a couple that haunt me: I invited this person over to my house, and even after the first encounter pushed the boundaries of what I was comfortable with, I invited him over again.

Experiencing sexual assault was alien and life-altering, and the act associated my understanding of sex with violence. As a fifteen-year-old new to sex and relationships, I struggled to make sense of the assault. I didn't have a framework to process what I experienced as related to rape culture. "Rape" was a term befitting of a legal procedural, not what happened in my bedroom. As a result, I characterized any of my experiences with sexual violence—ranging from street harassment to sexual assault—as less legitimate forms of violence. After all, I wasn't battered or bruised, or violently attacked by a stranger, so I believed my experiences couldn't be "legitimate" sexual assaults. Over time, I internalized social narratives about victim blaming. Those narratives eventually became part of my inner monologue.

I spent most of my high school years in a traumatized haze. Because I did not recognize my experience as sexual assault, I kept the experience secret and bore the pain alone. My physical appearance and disposition changed dramatically over the following months, and some of the choices I made during that period harmed myself and others. It took years, and the formation of community around survivorship, for me to understand how deeply sexual assault had affected me. I didn't tell anyone what happened to me until college—I could only face reality in a new context without reminders of the worst moment of my life.

As a teenager in the early-2000s, I didn't have language like consent, sexual assault, or rape culture through which to frame my experience. I rarely saw journalism that humanized a survivor's experience. I couldn't escape reminders of sexual assault. So how could I possibly understand what I had experienced? To do so, I delved into adolescent literature which contained myriad incidences of sexual assault.

Young Adult Literature and Rape Culture

YAL has been described by scholars as a critical point for initiating conversations about sexual violence and consent. Young adult literature (YAL) that meaningfully grapples with representation and complex social experiences can act as windows and mirrors for young readers (Bishop, 1990). The representative power of YAL to mirror youth identities can be extended to mirroring the internal experiences of youth survivors. Specifically, research has identified the power of YAL to spark meaningful conversations about rape culture and assault (Adams, 2020; Adams, 2021; Park, 2012; Malo-Juvera, 2014), and extant critical content analyses of YAL provide meaningful critique of representations of sexual assault in popular culture (Miller et al., 2023; Adams et al., 2022; Charles, 2019; Lewis, 2017; Lyons, 2022; Miller et al., 2022; Colantonio-Yurko et al., 2023).

Multiple scholars have discussed representations of victim-survivors (Moore, 2022) as well as their assailants (Miller et al., 2022). Indeed, many young adult novels addressing sexual assault address aspects of survivorship, often by drawing from critical feminist theory. For example, Miller and colleagues (2022) adapt Manne's (2019) constructs of "himpathy" and "herasure" to theorize how cultural narratives excuse and enable sexual violence, while Moore (2018a) draws from conceptions of childism(s) and shame resistance to theorize about the impacts of adult characters on the resilience of child survivors of sexual assault. Across these experiences, survivors are described as experiencing and resisting shame, fear, and anger—all of which are prevalent in non-fictionalized accounts of survivorship (Petrak, 2009). However, not all survivors will have the same degree of social support or be positioned the same way by their community (Miller et al., 2022; Moore, 2018a; White, 2020). Scholars indicate that depictions of survivorship in YAL ripple and bend around issues of intersectionality; both White (2020) and Khachab (2020) highlight the surveillance and othering of Muslim girls who encounter sexual violence, while Moore (2018a) highlights the social ostracization of a survivor assaulted by the son of a police officer. While YAL characters are often impacted by cultural narratives around victim blaming, reputation, and social positioning, these characters are also depicted as resisting rape culture. Harde (2023) describes these characters as enacting "justice brought about through deception and subterfuge by persisting girls" (p. 660). Similarly, Miller et al. (2022) identify thematic focuses on barriers to justice and vigilante justice across YAL; because cultural narratives around sexual assault so often lack justice, these imagined YAL texts depict resistance, agency, and advocacy. Throughout this body of scholarship, there is significant emphasis on cultural narratives about rape culture, and how these narratives impact the survivors depicted in YAL texts.

Recently, several scholars have highlighted the potentiality of YAL as a pedagogical avenue for interrupting rape culture (e.g., Adams, 2020; Colantonio-Yurko et al., 2018; Lyons, 2022; Malo-Juvera, 2014; Moore, 2021). Meaningful young adult texts that grapple with sexual assault have the potential to provide an imagined community for survivors: one in which they are not alone with their experiences. Charles (2019) characterizes characters in young adult literature as "companion[s] in acceptance and healing" as she saw her experiences mirrored through these novels. I too found what Charles (2019) characterized as "solace in silence" as I saw my experiences mirrored back to me by empathetic, well-rounded, courageous characters. Meanwhile, classroom discussions about incidences of sexual assault in canonical literature made my stomach twist, and I never mentioned my experiences during my own K-12 schooling.

As a classroom teacher, I wondered how many of my students experienced the familiar impact of sexual assault, and how many students struggled with the same sense of confusion, blame, self-trust, shame, and responsibility for their assault (Staller & Nelson-Gardell, 2005). Still, I balked at the idea of highlighting issues of sexual assault in the classroom. I recalled the white-hot prickle of shame that coursed through me during class discussion on any adjacent topic. I remembered how it felt to be an invisible survivor where no one knew I had been assaulted, yet I still experienced the after-shocks of sexual assault trauma (Schnittker, 2022). I longed to support my students without causing them to experience the fear and shame during classroom discussions that was an acute part of my experience.

Young Adult Texts as Windows and Mirrors into Survivors' Experiences

To that end, this chapter explores opportunities to disrupt the mental self-isolation experienced by young survivors of sexual assault by highlighting four young adult texts centered on experiences of sexual assault. Each text features unique internal and embodied experience of sexual assault that are both salient with my experiences as an adolescent survivor and could offer models for ways of being to adolescent victims I teach. It is my hope that this chapter will contribute to the efforts of teachers and teacher educators to provide critical literacy instruction regarding rape culture within secondary classrooms (Miller et al., 2023; Moore, 2021).

The Way I Used to Be

The Way I Used to Be by Amber Smith (2017) centers the victim's internal disorientation following sexual assault. This dislocation was the primary motivation for selecting this text: Eden, the protagonist, is a survivor who does not disclose the assault until the end of the novel. As Boehm and colleagues (2017) highlight, Eden's assailant is a school athlete, and is socially well-positioned. Eden lives, silently, in the assailant's golden shadow (Miller et al., 2022); therefore, the narration places significant emphasis on Eden's trauma and disorientation. This book offers an examination of invisible survivorship through Eden's emotional tumult, which may both resonate with and trouble readers.

The first chapter opens with Eden experiencing a flashback to her sexual assault at the hands of her brother's best friend during her freshman year of high school. And like many other young people—myself included—Eden did not report the incident to the police or disclose what happened to her parents, at least at first. The text's chapters, told in four parts that chronicle her freshman through senior year of high school, offer an unflinching examination of the shockwaves that sexual assault trauma can wreak on a young person's life.

The juxtaposition between Eden's inner world and how others perceive her is pronounced. Eden's brother says "You're not acting like yourself" (pg. 15), and her father calls her "melodramatic" (pg. 56), but the comments pale in comparison to Eden's inner turmoil. Within the first chapter, Eden says "I don't know that these images flashing through my mind—a movie of someone else, somewhere else—will never really go away, will never ever stop playing, will never stop haunting me" (p. 2). Eden describes the experience of being triggered:

> All can I hear is my blood rushing and my heart drumming in my ears. A pulsing in my throat, like there's a big jumbled ball of words stuck in there dying to get out. He puts both arms around me. But I feel suffocated. Don't want to be held. Don't want to be touched. Not by anyone ever again in my entire life (pg. 295).

Eden experiences swirling self-doubt and frustration over what she perceives as her own passivity; she is gripped with guilt over not saying "no" or fighting back against the assault. Yet she also explodes in violent anger when triggered. When Eden learns that her assailant's sister is spreading rumors about Eden sleeping with her brother, she reacts violently:

> I feel something savage and electrical flow through me, like my hands could strangle her, like they're controlled by some part of my brain that's immune to logic, the same part of my brain that's allowing me to say these things, these fucked-up things that are just going to give me away. I could just . . . my hands. Reach out. God. For anything. To hurt. Next thing I know she's on the floor. (pp. 309-310).

Despite her deep distress, Eden fights to appear normal while combating an inner belief that she is indelibly tainted by the violence she experienced.

Eden transforms her physical appearance in an identity reformulation that distances her from her past self, a self who was assaulted. She says "It's simple really. All you have to do is act like you're normal and okay, and people start treating you that way" (p. 66). As Eden tries to reinvent herself, to become someone who this assault had never happened to, the feelings of shame, confusion, anger, and disorientation continuously color her narration. Tendrils of rape culture envelop Eden's self-talk, ranging from slut shaming ("I know that everyone thinks I'm a slut and I probably am," p. 346) to victim blaming ("And maybe it was essentially all my fault for acting like I liked him, for actually liking him," p. 148).

Moments of this book were challenging for me to read because they were so adjacent to my own experience. Eden's desperation to change her identity, her frustration with her parents and herself, her incandescent rage and deep distress; these aspects of Eden's inner world mirrored my experiences as a pre-disclosure teen survivor. The changes in Eden's personality—violent outbursts, identity shifts—are characterized by adults in the book as teenage hormones, and by Eden's friends as unhealthy behaviors, but I found these actions familiar. Smith's vivid descriptions of internal confusion and behaviors that defy explanation, even for Eden herself, reflected experiences of discombobulation and confusion that can occur following sexual assault (Petrak, 2009).

Exit, Pursued by a Bear

Unlike other texts in this chapter, E. K. Johnston's *Exit, Pursued by a Bear* (2016) features a survivor who is, by virtue of the nature of the assault, unable to be invisible. In part, this is a feature of the source material, Shakespeare's *A Winter's Tale*, but this visibility offers a unique portrait of survivorship. Hermione Winters is popular, an excellent athlete, and a leader on her cheerleading team. Yet, after she wakes up in the hospital, she realizes that she was assaulted while realizing simultaneously that her assault is public knowledge. This book highlighted that not all survivors have the capacity to remain invisible—while also disrupting typical narratives around shame resulting from sexual assault (Moore, 2018a). Hermione Winters is the kind of survivor I wish I had read about as a teenager; she oozes competence and clarity. Her self-conception is clear, and her community supports her following the assault; Hermione doesn't experience the identity interruption highlighted in *The Way I Used To Be*, for example. This book expands narratives of sexual assault survivorship to emphasize community, support, and confidence.

The first five chapters depict Hermione at her best: she's popular, an excellent athlete, and a leader on her team. During the sixth chapter, at a cheer camp party she attended with her friends and boyfriend, she is drugged and raped. When she wakes up in the hospital, she's lost twelve hours of her life, and everyone in her small community seems to know about her assault. She is slut-shamed by her boyfriend—a fellow athlete—and rumors fly on social media, yet she still doesn't know her assailant. Hermione experiences a familiar fear: that this assault is now all she will be remembered for. Yet she responds assertively, telling her teammates how to support her, publicly breaking up with her boyfriend, and advocating for herself to therapists and police. When Hermione's post-assault pregnancy test comes back positive, Hermione says with determination, "I will not be the class pregnancy" (p. 117). Her choice to terminate her pregnancy is practical and Johnston depicts the abortion with profound empathy.

More uniquely, Hermione's surrounding community largely validates her experiences, from the police officers to her reverend. Moore (2018a, 2018b) analyzes Hermione's community of support within her spatial context, highlighting that Hermione's family rallies around her in shared vulnerability and support (2018a), but even this exceptionally supportive community—and her community of fellow athletes (Boehm et al., 2017)—cannot fully mitigate the flashbacks that emerge when Hermione revisits the site of her assault (2018b). Hermione experiences traumatic flashbacks and spikes of fear, yet is supported by a strong network of friends, mentors, and family. She regularly discusses her assault with guidance counselors, friends, and family, and when questioned about why she's doing so well, Hermione reports "I think it's because I don't remember... Right now it's like it happened—like another person was raped" (p. 102). When her boyfriend spreads rumors about Hermione's assault, she's able to proclaim publicly that "If you think I'm going to apologize for being drugged and raped, you have another thing coming" (pg. 104). Much like the character Hermione in Shakespeare's *The Winter's Tale*, Hermione is righteous and strong; even when falsely accused of infidelity, her grace never wavers. Hermione Winters shows similar resolve in the face of public knowledge of her assault. When she experiences flashbacks, terror, moments of rage, her support networks rise to the challenge: her friends pull Hermione to safety and call her therapist.

Yet Hermione's experience of assault may not be as common for many readers. In an author's note, Johnston speaks to the degree of support Hermione receives:

> It was very important to me that Hermione have an excellent support system in this book. Her parents, friends, teachers, coach, minister, and community rally around her. She receives the medical care she requires. The police are gracious and helpful. This is not standard procedure. Many rape victims are isolated, unable to ask for the help they need, much less receive it. (p. 247)

This author's note problematizes the imagined reality of the novel, while also treating Hermione's character with consideration. Yet some survivors may read the novel without similar support in their own lives. Although Hermione asserts her blamelessness with dignity, some survivors may not have the ability or desire to publicly defend themselves. This book may be useful for survivors as well as those looking to support survivors, such as a parent or friend.

Foul is Fair

Playing off of the themes of betrayal, vengeance, and murder found in Shakespeare's *Macbeth*, Hannah Capin's (2020) *Foul is Fair* plays on the rage and thirst for justice for survivors. *Foul is Fair* begins with Elizabeth Jade Khanjara, called "Elle" before the events of the plot truly begin, attending a party thrown by students at a nearby elite prep school. After being drugged and raped at a private school party by a group of wealthy boys and their co-conspirators, Elle changes her name to Jade and fixates on revenge towards every person involved in her assault. Cold, calculating rage characterizes Jade's inner experience following her assault. Through this characterization, *Foul is Fair* complicates the dominant dichotomy of victimhood and survivorship. Both terms "victim" and "survivor" evoke passivity from the recipient of the violence, and Jade immediately rejects this reconstruction of her identity as passive.

As Miller and colleagues (2022) identify, Jade's friends and family express a type of "hopeless support" (p. 311) following Jade's assault that recognizes the systemic barriers to justice for sexual assault survivors. The impracticality of legal support leads Jade and her friends to persist towards justice through what Harde (2023) describes as "deception and subterfuge" (p. 660). Jade refuses to be defined in discourses of weakness, victimhood, or even survivor. When the hospital therapist asks Jade what word she'd prefer, her friends sing as a chorus of witches through the group chat: "Tell her queen… Tell her killer… Tell her justice" (p. 16). Finally, Jade responds with a "lethal" smile: "I mean those boys didn't turn me into anything I wasn't before… But I would prefer… Avenger" (p. 16).

Yet Jade's rejection of the victim/survivor dichotomy does not mean that Jade circumvents the after-effects of trauma. Directly following her assault, Jade dramatically alters her identity: she changes her name from Elle to Jade, re-dyes her bleached blonde hair to black, and never again wears the jade-colored contacts she wore to the party. Later, Duncan corners Jade and grabs her arm tightly, and she flashes back to the moment of assault. These triggers seem to frustrate Jade as much as motivate her. Throughout the novel, Jade never imagines her life after the culmination of her revenge scheme, almost as if the potentiality of her future has been erased along with "Elle." In contrast, Jade has one purpose: to avenge the girl she was before her choices and freedom were taken away from her. The book ends on a triumphant note of vengeance, but there's no implication of a future for Jade. Her role is accomplished.

From the perspective of survivorship, Jade embodies the incandescent rage that can accompany sexual assault. These is no singular essentialist experience of the psychological impact(s) of a sexual assault (Schnittker, 2022); however, it is worth highlighting that sexual assault is a violent crime committed against a person's physical body with severe mental and emotional impacts. Scholarship has characterized rape as a "spiritual death," (Messina-Dysert, 2012) and international law has declared rape as a "crime against humanity" and an "act of torture" (Gorman, 2016, p. 1). Therefore, it's worth considering Jade's rage and desire for vengeance as an entirely understandable response.

Jade feels rage like it's in her bloodstream. When I read *Foul is Fair*, I felt her rage along with her. As a young survivor, I was too deep in shame to feel protective over myself. In contrast, Jade never feels shame; she's defiant, she's enraged, she's protective towards herself. She views what happened to her as a crime in which society is complicit. A dose of this rage might have counteracted the shame and self-blame I sat within as a teenager. While other books covered in this chapter provide identity models for moving on from an assault, *Foul is Fair* sinks deeply into rage as a defense of the self. Jade's violence is *revenge*: despite her defiance that her identity wasn't changed by the assault, she seeks vengeance for a severe and life-altering crime. Jade is cruel, savage, deliberate, intentional; she is clearly a fictionalized character from a tragedy. But her rage is real. There is a satisfaction in knowing that Jade obtained the vengeance she sought; however, her actions are not designed as models for young readers. Instead, Jade's rage provides literary space for readers to connect with that rage within themselves. *Foul is Fair* provides an imagined space for vengeance as a counter to the narrative paralysis of an assault.

Saints and Misfits

In *Saints and Misfits* (2017), S.K. Ali addresses large concepts of othering, surveillance, consent, and religious community through a raw depiction of Janna's life following a sexual assault. *Saints and Misfits* centers a female Muslim protagonist who is repeatedly othered and harmed by the cultural divisions between her religious community and her secular school community. Miller et al. (2022) critically analyzed this text for themes regarding depictions of sexual assault, and White (2020) and Khachab (2020) both addressed othering and religious marginalization in community responses to Janna's body.

In S. K. Ali's (2017) *Saints and Misfits*, Janna Yusuf categorizes people in her life into three categories: saints, misfits, and monsters. As a young Muslim who recently started wearing hijab, Janna identifies many members of her faith and school communities as saints, and labels those who drift between communities as misfits. But monsters lurk everywhere. In Janna's case, the monster is Farooq, who constantly lurks at the periphery of Janna's life: her brother's friend, her friend Fizz's cousin, he attends her school, and he is well positioned in her mosque. Farooq had assaulted Janna prior to the events of the novel, and Farooq's significant social standing in their religious community compelled Janna to hide the assault. White (2020) frames Farooq as isolating Janna in a "liminal space" (p. 130): Farooq's social power combined with Janna's visibility in her school community make her vulnerable to exclusion if she divulges the assault. Both White (2020) and Khachab (2020) emphasize the visibility and surveillance Janna experiences as a young woman in hijab in American schools, with both scholars noting widespread interest in examining her body and challenging her agency regarding her clothing. Janna is repeatedly othered by non-Muslim friends and classmates, and this othering extends to cyberbullying. All the while, Farooq continues to stalk the boundaries of Janna's life, at times taking advantage of Janna's othering from both secular and religious communities to isolate her. Throughout the novel, Janna navigates intercultural relationships and harassment regarding her modesty at school, yet Muslim characters regularly discuss modesty from the perspective of self-actualization and control over access to oneself.

Farooq's assault on Janna violated her modesty, but he was interrupted before the assault progressed. As a result, the book places emphasis on evidence. How can one prove the assault took place without a witness, body fluids, or evidence of physical harm? When Janna tells her cousin about Farooq's assault, she doesn't believe her. When Janna anonymously writes to her uncle's advice column, his response also emphasized the importance of evidence. Janna's friend Sausun wanted to confront Farooq to prove that he committed the assault. This is a point of tension for Janna, who wants her newfound ability to confront Farooq to be enough. But Sausun repeatedly returns to the sociocultural systems that protect assaulters and asserts that it is, unfortunately, Janna's responsibility to prove Farooq was a monster. The ambiance of rape culture—and that a survivor is unlikely to be believed without proof—pervade the narrative in what Miller and colleagues (2022) characterize as "hopeless support" (p. 311).

Farooq stalks Janna—she uses the verb "creep" to describe his surveillance—both at school and at mosque-sponsored events. He consistently tries to approach Janna to get her alone, attempting to violate her modesty again. He takes pictures of her at various events, even escalating to share pictures of Janna without a hijab online while moralizing about immodesty, thus violating Janna's modesty again. Farooq tells Janna's crush that Farooq and Janna are dating, while simultaneously sending a picture of Janna and her crush to Janna's family to destroy her reputation. And these actions are framed by Farooq insisting "I just want to talk to you" (pg. 207). These actions serve to silence Janna, yet she subverts this silencing through a public accusation while wearing a niqab. This confrontation somehow cleansed her: "The disgust I feel *at me* is gone. The gunk of self-blame dissolves to leave just me standing there" (pg. 305). Her resistance is embedded within her self-presentation; her modesty is a reclamation of her agency.

In the other novels, the assailants appear to view the survivors as disposable, enacted by ignoring, threatening, or obscuring their identity. Farooq is a different kind of assailant: one who wants to control or even possess Janna. As a reader-survivor, I found myself experiencing strong physiological responses to Farooq's harassment, such as breathlessness and an elevated heart rate. Whenever Janna was starting to feel confident or explore her own identity, I began to anticipate Farooq's appearance. His constant presence left me empathizing with the emotional weight that Farooq's stalking had on Janna. In particular, one scene where Farooq corners Janna after the Quiz Game causes me to feel an intense physical empathetic reaction. Farooq's constant presence cast a shadow over all other events in the book, and the fear that runs through Janna's otherwise-typical high school experiences was palpable. Yet, while Farooq forced Janna into a vulnerable position between two communities, Janna used her marginalization as a vehicle for self-actualization— by speaking up, and by being believed.

Discussion: Supporting Survivors Learning About Rape Culture

Alongside other scholars, I echo the call for the interrogation of rape culture, particularly through the lens of YAL, and that the quality of representation of sexual assault in adolescent texts merits consideration (Charles, 2019; Colantonio-Yurko et al., 2023; Lewis, 2017; Miller et al., 2023). In this chapter, I have presented descriptions of survivorship as conveyed in four young adult novels that center the fallout from incidences of sexual assault. Each character had markedly different experiences with and responses to the violence they experienced, thus presenting readers with different depictions of survivorship. My intention was to explore the inner experience of each protagonist through the lens of a survivor-reader, including my embodied and cognitive responses to each narrativization, to explore the varied dimensions of survivorship. Because these texts either begin with or include the incident of assault described, the reader witnesses characters move through the stages of sexual assault disclosure identified by Staller and Nelson-Gardell (2005). Each character moves through a version of the self-phase and experiences the sense of isolation and internal disorientation that occurs after a sexual assault. Focusing on commonalities and differences across experiences of survivorship in YAL may problematize the depiction of survivorship as an essentialist experience. Some survivors disclose their assault, while others don't. Some survivors seek distance from the incident, while others seek revenge. Yet all characters were indelibly changed by the assault, with side effects ranging from disturbed sleep, to panic attacks, to unpredictable flashbacks.

Across all four novels, all four characters fought to reassert control over their lives: Eden and Jade attempt to re-fashion their identities while Hermione and Janna fight for normalcy. All characters were depicted as living complex, full lives throughout their books, although the trauma of their assault affected each character differently. Characters express anger in socially acceptable ways—such as Hermione's confrontation with her boyfriend and Janna's confrontation of her assailant—and unacceptable ways, such as murder or physical violence; yet all four characters experience anger. All characters felt the public eye of rape culture surveilling them: Janna's concern over evidence and being believed, the erasure of Hermione's identity other than her assault, Eden's belief that she deserved what happened to her. Eden, Hermione, Jade, and Janna are all depicted as brave young women reclaiming agency after sexual assault, yet their experiences and responses are as varied as the stories they're situated within. For specific themes and sample discussion questions for survivorship as depicted in each book (see Table 2.1).

Instructional Risks and Strategies

Sexual assault is a challenging and painfully personal topic for many readers, both adolescent and adult. Yet this challenge can provide windows into the experiences of sexual assault survivorship, or mirrors for students who may have survived sexual violence themselves (Bishop, 1990). However, extreme care must be taken towards young readers, particularly those who may be survivors of sexual assault themselves. Some students may or may not be prepared to discuss their own experience, or students may be impacted by classroom discussion of sexual assault. I echo other scholars promoting considerations for teaching about sexual assault in classrooms (e.g., Miller et al., 2023; Adams et al., 2022; Colantonio-Yurko et al., 2018). To that end, I highlight three risks involved in classroom learning regarding discussions of sexual assault or sexual assault survivorship, alongside practical considerations that might mitigate this risk when teaching content containing sexual assault.

Risk 1: Unexpected content pertaining to sexual assault.

In *The Way I Used to Be*, Eden flinches when the word rape comes up during coursework, but hides her reaction (Smith, 2016, p. 28); in *Saints and Misfits*, Janna can only focus on Caliban's attempted assault in *The Tempest* during her English class(Ali, 2018, p. 95). Like Janna and Eden, invisible survivors in classrooms may experience similar discomfort when incidences of sexual violence occur without advance warning. Indeed, Moore (2022) indicates, schools might

Table 2.1 Sample Text Themes and Survivorship Questions

	Sample Themes	Sample Survivorship Questions
The Way I Used to Be	• Responses to trauma • Identity change • Self-actualization	• How are Eden's inner experiences and public behavior similar? How are they different? • Track how Eden changes throughout the novel. How does her change indicate personal growth?
Exit, Pursued by a Bear	• Stigma and rumor • Communities of care • Resilience	• How does Hermione's community support her throughout the novel? • Compare and contrast public response to Hermione's assault to Hermione's self-perception. What similarities and differences do you notice?
Foul is Fair	• Enabling rape culture • "Golden Boy" tropes • Vengeance	• How is Jade emotionally impacted by her assault? How does her emotional experience emerge in her behavior? • Why does Jade separate herself from Elle? Discuss how these two facets of Jade's personality highlight her emotional experience.
Saints and Misfits	• Evidence and proof • Sexual justice activism • Agency	• Why is Janna so focused on the idea of evidence and proof? What evidence of sexual assault do the characters perceive as credible? • How does Janna use her Hijab and Niqab to express her agency?

not be safe locations for survivors of sexual violence, as sexual violence can be carried out on school campuses. However, thoughtfully raising issues of sexual violence in classroom environments can provide a signal of safety to students.

To mitigate the risk of unexpected content depicting sexual violence, consider providing trigger or content warnings for depictions or incidences of sexual violence (Colantonio-Yurko et al., 2018). Effectively providing content warnings requires attunement to the macro and micro ways in which sexual violence occurs in class texts beyond explicit instances of assault. I provide overall warnings at the beginning of a novel centering sexual assault, and warnings for chapters containing explicit depictions, so readers can warn themselves in advance or skip relevant pages. Additionally, educators should consider the home experiences of students, and be sure to communicate with caregivers regarding content containing sexual violence. I provide overall warnings at the beginning of a novel centering sexual assault, and warnings for chapters containing explicit depictions, so readers can warn themselves in advance or skip relevant pages. Additionally, educators should consider the home experiences of students, and be sure to communicate with caregivers regarding content containing sexual violence.

Risk 2: Classroom discussions that trivialize the experience of sexual assault survivorship.

While classroom discussions on rape culture have the potential to be highly meaningful for adolescent learners, there is always the risk that classrooms discussions could trivialize or dismiss instances of sexual assault. Even if no students in a classroom have disclosed an assault, it is likely that there will be survivors of sexual assault in any classroom full of teenagers. Furthermore, it's worth considering that there is the possibility that these discussions could be taking place in a classroom including a survivor and a perpetrator; Janna, Eden, and Jade all attended school with their assailants.

To mitigate harmful comments during classroom discussions on rape culture, these discussions should be established with existing norms such as defining rape culture (Miller et al., 2023; Colantonio-Yurko et al., 2023; Colantonio-Yurko et al., 2018) and naming components of rape culture such as victim blaming. In Moore's (2022) examination of teaching about rape in ELA classrooms, she highlighted considerations around defining the experience of "triggers" in a non-trivializing way as part of cultivating a respectful environment. Additionally, students may benefit from alternative assignments for class discussions that students can select without explanation, such as journal responses or creative responses, as well as the opportunity to leave the room without explanation if needed (Moore, 2022). Additionally, when covering material that addresses sexual assault, provide students with support resources: informational materials, hotlines, and guidance counselor support may all be relevant.

Risk 3: Misunderstanding of the responses of survivors.

Although the four books addressed in this chapter provide insight into some psychological responses of sexual assault survivors, some readers may struggle to empathize with a survivor's behavior. While challenging, exploring texts such as those featured in this chapter with youth bears the potential to provide windows into the experiences of sexual assault survivorship, or mirrors for students who may have survived violence themselves.

Survivors of sexual assault may not act in "expected" ways, especially if those expectations are conveyed through dominant narratives. Educators should avoid describing survivor character psychology as abnormal; indeed, it may be worthwhile to examine resources on responses to sexual assault with students to provide insight into responses to trauma. Part of this examination may involve focusing on the experience of trauma triggers by attending to differences and commonalities across survivors in YAL texts like these. For example, do Jade's trauma triggers look like Eden's? Understanding the responses of sexual assault survivors means understanding that survivorship is not an essentialist experience; while there may be commonalities, survivors are unique, and their trauma may manifest uniquely.

Conclusion

This is the most vulnerable piece of public writing I've ever produced. As a literacy scholar and a teacher educator, I regularly write about critical concerns. Yet, even after fifteen years, I still feel a silent shame around disclosure of sexual assault. The idea of associating my professional identity with my assault is intimidating, and even more so within an educational context. Historically, when topics of sexual assault were raised and abstracted in school settings, I experienced mental and physiological symptoms that, like these characters, ranged widely from rage to disassociation. Yet, as I got to know these characters, I couldn't help but reflect upon their survivorship. I was struck by how many of their experiences resonated with my own, and I could only postulate that similar resonance might be experienced by student readers, some of whom may be invisible survivors themselves.

Young adult literature helped me understand sexual assault before I had language or context for what happened to me. Texts like the above, which contain well-researched and meaningful representations of sexual assault survivorship, are the kinds of texts that I can imagine resonating with as a young and undisclosed survivor. It's books like these that made me feel like I wasn't alone.

Literature Cited

Ali, S. K. (2018). *Saints and misfits*. Salaam Reads.
Capin, H. (2020). *Foul is fair*. Wednesday Books.
Johnston, E. K. (2017). *Exit, pursued by a bear*. Penguin Books.
Shakespeare, W. (2017). *Winter's tale*. Penguin Publishing Group.
Shakespeare, W. (2000/1606). *Macbeth*. https://www.bartleby.com/lit-hub/the-oxford-shakespeare/macbeth-by-william-shakespear
Smith, A. (2016). *The way I used to be*. Margaret K. McElderry Books.

References

Adams, B. (2020). "I didn't feel confident talking about this issue... but I knew I could talk about a book": Using young adult literature to make sense of #metoo. *Journal of Literacy Research, 52*(2), 209-230.

Adams, B. (2021). Consent is not as simple as tea: Student activism against rape culture. *Girlhood Studies, 14*(1), 1-18.

Adams, B., Colantonio-Yurko, K., Miller, H. C. & Boehm, S. M. (2022). Beyond perpetrators, victims, and survivors: young adult literature as bystander intervention education. *The ALAN Review, 49*(3), 42-52.

Bishop R. S. (1990). Mirrors, windows, and sliding glass doors. *Perspectives, 6*(3), ix-xi.

Charles, A. (2019). Sexual assault and its impacts in young adult literature. *Criterion: A Journal of Literary Criticism, 12*(2), 97-103.

Colantonio-Yurko, K. C., Adams, B., Boehm, S., & Miller, H. C. (2023). Boundaries, objectification, and gender norms: Addressing sexual and gender-based harassment with middle grade literature. *Middle School Journal, 54*(1), 23-31.

Colantonio-Yurko, K., Miller, H. C., & Cheveallier, J. (2018). "But she didn't scream": Teaching about sexual assault in young adult literature. *Journal of Language and Literacy Education, 14*(1), 1-16.

Gorman, L. (2016). Rape as torture: Application of the U.S. torture statute to the physical and psychological consequences of rape and sexual violence on victims. *Stanford Law School: Law and Policy Lab.* https://law.stanford.edu/publications/rape-as-torture-application-of-the-u-s-torture-statute-to-the-physical-and-psychological-consequences-of-rape-and-sexual-violence-on-victims/

Harde, R. (2023). "What about justice?": Persisting girls in young adult rape fiction. *Women's Studies, 52*(6), 660-673.

Khachab, N. (2020). Freak show: Religiously marginalized female bodies as spectacle in second-generation literature. *Children's Literature Association Quarterly, 45*(1), 4-24.

Lewis, K. (2017). *She wanted it?: Examining young adult literature and its portrayals of rape culture* (Publication No. 10262058) [Thesis, Illinois State University]. ProQuest Dissertations & Theses Global.

Lyons, K. (2022). *If it's not yes, it's no: Examining and understanding sexual dominance in young adult literature and how to teach it critically* (Publication No. 29395971) [Dissertation, University of La Verne]. ProQuest Dissertations & Theses Global.

Manne, K. (2019). *Down girl: The logic of misogyny.* Oxford University Press.

Malo-Juvera, V. (2014). *Speak*: The effect of literacy instruction on adolescents' rape myth acceptance. *Research in the Teaching of English, 48*(4), 407-427.

Messina-Dysert, G. (2012). Rape and spiritual death. *Feminist Theology, 20*(2), 120-132.

Miller, H. C., Boehm, S., Colantonio-Yurko, K., Adams, B., & Mertens, G. (2023). Naming and challenging rape culture in english curriculum: a framework for teaching canonical texts with contemporary adaptations. *Changing English, 30*(2), 117-129.

Miller, H. C., Boehm, S., Colantonio-Yurko, K., & Adams, B. (2022). Himpathy, herasure, and down girl moves: A critical content analysis of sexual assault in young adult literature. *Journal of Literacy Research, 54*(3), 298-321.

Moore, A. (2022). Representations of testimonial smothering and critical witnessing of rape victim-survivors in Laurie Halse Anderson's *Speak* fanfiction. *Children's Literature in Education, 55*, 162-178.

Moore, A. (2021). Safe space(s), content (trigger) warnings, and being 'care-ful' with trauma literature pedagogy and rape culture in secondary English teacher education. *Changing English, 29*(1), 77-88.

Moore, A. (2018a). "I knew you were trouble": Considering childism(s), shame resilience, and adult caretaker characters surrounding YA rape survivor protagonists. *New Review of Children's Literature and Librarianship, 24*(2), 144-166.

Moore, A. (2018b). Traumatic geographies: Mapping the violent landscapes driving YA rape survivors indoors in Laurie Halse Anderson's *Speak*, Elizabeth Scott's *Living Dead Girl*, and E.K. Johnston's *Exit, Pursued by a Bear*. *Jeunesse: Young People, Texts, Cultures, 10*(1), 58-84.

National Sexual Violence Resource Center (NSVRC). (2018). *Teenagers & sexual violence*. https://www.nsvrc.org/sites/default/files/publications/2019-02/Teenagers_508.pdf

Park, J. Y. (2012). Re-imaging reader-response in middle and secondary schools: Early adolescent girls' critical and communal reader responses to the young adult novel *Speak*. *Children's Literature in Education, 43*(3), 191-212.

Petrak, J. (2009). The psychological impact of sexual assault. In Petrak J. & Hedge, B. (Eds.), *The trauma of sexual assault: Treatment, prevention, and practice* (pp. 21-43). Wiley.

Schnittker, J. (2022). What makes sexual violence different? Comparing the effects of sexual and non-sexual violence on psychological distress. *SSM - Mental Health, 2*, 100115.

Staller, K. M., & Nelson-Gardell, D. (2005). "A burden in your heart": Lessons of disclosure from female preadolescent and adolescent survivors of sexual abuse. *Child Abuse & Neglect, 29*(12), 1415-1432.

White, L. (2020). Negotiating the hyphens in a culture of surveillance: Embodied surveillance and the representation of Muslim adolescence in angelophone YA fiction. *Jeunesse: Young People, Texts, Cultures, 12*(1), 122-143.

The Sharp Edge of Silence: Using a Young Adult Novel to C.A.R.E. For Students

Emily Pendergrass, Vanderbilt University, Melanie Hundley, Vanderbilt University, Michael Neel, Vanderbilt University, and Kathryn Pendergrss, Lewis and Clark College

Eighteen seniors drift into class, chatting about our day, and we find our seats. A single piece of paper sits on each desk. The teacher asks us to read two paragraphs as preparation for a silent discussion. There is no talking at all. In this silent discussion, each student writes something we are feeling about the content of the reading on a blank piece of paper before passing it to our right. Each member of the group reads what is written on the paper, writes a response, and continues passing to their right until the paper has moved all the way around the circle back to the original writer. Once you have your paper back, you read how your classmates responded to you. We then discuss in small groups focusing on something that stood out or something that a classmate said that surprised us. Today, the topic of discussion was 'The Continued Failure to Tackle Rape Culture within Schools.'

Kat's (author 4) memory shared in the above vignette, demonstrates a complicated issue. While the subject of the discussion, rape culture, is an important topic for adolescents to discuss, it was made more difficult by three things. First, this conversation occurred just two weeks into the school year, a time where there was not an established classroom community. Second, there was not adequate instructional preparation or support for the discussion. Finally, the teacher was not a participant in the group discussion to mitigate harm.

When reading Kat's reflections, the other authors of this chapter raised concerns about the directions, or lack thereof, given for the assignment. *What were the parameters for the discussion? Were there guidelines?* Kat explained that there were no guidelines beyond the directions given. Kat shared with co-authors that the ensuing discussion resulted in tears because one of her peers said, "*We can't do anything to stop rape culture because we are just teenagers. It's just how life is. It's a fact of life. I am just a 17-year-old guy; there's nothing I can do.*" Kat and the student had an exchange in which Kat characterized the student's lack of desire to intervene in rape culture as: "*being complicit with rape culture.*" This statement resulted in classroom chaos, as other students jumped in to defend Kat's peer.

Inspired by Kat's experience in her secondary English classroom, this chapter offers guidance for engaging in conversations around rape culture and sexual assault with adolescents. As teachers, we recognize the need to engage in critical discussions about rape and understand the complexity and detail needed in planning for difficult discussions with students. As part of this chapter, we introduce a framework for supporting students as they engage critically and empathetically with complex issues. We align ourselves with scholars who take up young adult literature (YAL) in the classroom to challenge societal stereotypes and cultural norms that perpetuate rape culture and provides a platform for brave spaces in classrooms (Curwood, 2013; Colantonio-Yurko et al., 2023; Moore, 2024; Storer & Strohl, 2017). In this chapter, we use a young adult (YA) novel, *The Sharp Edge of Silence* (Rosenblum, 2023), as a curricular example for educators. We demonstrate how to establish an ethic of care for students (Noddings, 2012) and use this YA text as a way to develop common language with expectations for having difficult conversations in classrooms. The issues addressed in *The Sharp Edge of Silence* mirror many of the same issues that we see in society in regards to rape culture. Centering the discussions around a specific text allows for layered conversations and develops a more complex understanding of the issue.

Rape Culture and Text

Rape culture, a term that first appeared in the 1970s, was a term used to describe a society in which rape and sexual violence is considered commonplace and accepted as "the consummate act of male power in a culture of patriarchy" (Peters & Besley, 2019, p. 460.) This definition draws attention to the ways in which rape and sexual assault are not about sex and rather about power and dominance. Herb (2021) argued that rape culture "can be defined as the social and environmental structures, commonly stemming from patriarchal or misogynistic ideologies, that contribute to creating a culture of normalizing, trivializing, and enabling sexual assault" (pp. 69-70). This becomes an important term to think about and unpack as teachers consider the group with which they work, the structures of schools, and statistics of sexual assaults reported for middle and high school age students.

According to the statstics, youth aged 14 to 17 are in the highest risk category for sexual violence, with more than one in four adolescents (27.3%) having been sexually victimized during their lifetimes; however, this number is likely higher since it is estimated that only 19% of assaults are reported (Kualdi, 2023). The Rape, Abuse & Incest National Network (n.d.) provides additional nuance for this statistic by reporting that girls and women ages 16-19 are 4 times more likely than the general population to experience rape, attempted rape, or sexual assault. Statistics alone will not create change; for empathy and change to happen, we must rely on stories (see Polletta et al., 2011). Malo-Juvera (2014) notes,

" Rape is a traumatic event and often entails both physical injuries; moreover, the devastating psychological effects may lack of help-seeking behavior" (p. 411). The difficulty of navigating asking for help is only one part of why it is critical that teachers provide access to difficult social issues. Narratives play a crucial role in shaping our identities, both individually and collectively. They serve as a medium through which we can explore the past, imagine the future, and make sense of our experiences. Moreover, narratives are instrumental in cultivating empathy. They enable us to witness and understand events and experiences beyond our own direct encounters (Gee, 2017). This is especially important when navigating challenging social issues with young people (Adams, 2020). Many educators turn to YAL for this purpose. YAL engages with ideas, social concerns, and actions that affect the lives of its readers. As such, this field of literature has the power to shape perceptions, challenge societal norms, and address pressing issues.

Narratives featuring diverse characters and gender roles can disrupt traditional expectations and foster critical thinking (Alsup, 2015). By incorporating themes like power and gender dynamics into classroom curricula, educators can create brave spaces for dialogue and education (Arao & Clemens, 2013). *The Sharp Edge of Silence* (Rosenblum, 2023), introduced below, provides a nuanced story that looks at the struggles of the survivors, the difficulties of the support systems, and the challenges of changing a school culture. This novel, like much YAL, is a tool that educators can use to facilitated discussions among adolescents around rape culture and sexual violence.

Discussion, Difficult Topics, and YAL

Adolescents may lack the language, development, and skills to know how to ask for help, respond to questions, deal with their emotions, and engage with others about what has happened to them (van den Toren et al., 2019). While this may be the case in some instances, we have found that adolescents have a range of skills they can rely on if given some guidance. For example, support from the teacher in the initial conversation could have shown the students how to determine the level of power they have in a situation or how to counter inappropriate or uncomfortable jokes. Rape culture encompasses the normalization and perpetuation of attitudes and behaviors that trivialize, encourage, or justify sexual violence (Herb, 2021). Drawing attention to instances in a classroom discussion that perpetuates this normalization may be a tool to help students disrupt this narrative. This chapter aims to explore teachers' preparation to dive into the complex issues associated with rape and rape culture, how YAL represents and addresses rape culture, while examining its impact on readers' understanding and awareness of this difficult topic.

One challenge for educators then becomes how to create spaces for dialogue particularly in the middle or high school classroom. For example, how does one talk with an adolescent about consent? Righi et al. (2021) argued that there is a "paucity of research on consent among high school-age adolescents compared with the research on college-age populations" (p. 15). This lack of research illustrates one of the hurdles that educators face in that it shows how little is known about this topic in relation to high school students. Righi et al. (2021) noted that adolescents primarily defined consent as verbal permission to engage in sexual activity while also noting that "through a verbal standard of affirmative consent, they suggested that—in practice—sexual consent was more likely to be conveyed through nonverbal cues, especially through silence or the absence of a verbal refusal of sexual activity (i.e., saying "no")" (p. 305). This is important because what it shows is that while adolescents understand the need for both parties to verbally consent to engage in sexual activities, consent and what counts as consent gets confusing when put into actual practice (Righi et al., 2021). Additionally, Righi et al. (2021) note that adolescents "described girls as being primarily responsible for communicating consent to sexual activity, such that the absence of sexual refusal by a girl was considered a sign of sexual consent" (p. 302). The lack of clarity around consent and responsibility is just one of the issues that educators face when talking about issues of rape, sexual assault, and rape culture.

YAL does not shy away from exploring rape, sexual assault, and rape culture. While many may consider this topic too painful or difficult for adolescent readers, adolescents themselves recognize the need for these texts. For example, sixteen-year-old Sarah, a former student of the second author, read Anderson's (1999) *Speak* and said, "This book saved my life. I thought I was the only one." YAL provides numerous representations of rape or rape culture illuminating its existence and impact on individuals and communities. Seminal works like the aforementioned *Speak* and more recently, O'Neill's (2015) *Asking For It* explore themes of victim-blaming, consent, and the silencing of survivors, providing readers with a profound insight into the realities of rape culture. These narratives, and many others like them, challenge readers to critically examine cultural norms and question the inherent biases that perpetuate such attitudes.

Author Positionalities

The first author is a white woman and the mother of the fourth author, Kat. The fourth author is a white woman and undergraduate studying biology. The second author is also a white woman and the fourth a white male. Race and gender are critical factors when discussing rape culture, as they influence the experiences and perceptions of sexual violence. Marginalized racial and gender groups face unique challenges and stigmas, and their stories are often disregarded or misunderstood. Acknowledging these differences is essential for creating inclusive and comprehensive educational materials.

The first three authors have worked alongside many students of all ages who have survived sexual violence and have learned/are continuing to learn the delicate work of supporting students after difficult times. As white scholars, we recognize that our privileged identities inform our work in young adult literature by shaping our perspectives, influencing our interpretations, and impacting the ways we engage with and present complex issues such as rape culture, race, and gender. Our backgrounds afford us certain viewpoints and access to resources that can both enrich our understanding and inadvertently shield us from the full spectrum of experiences represented in YAL. This awareness drives us to consciously reflect on our biases, actively seek diverse voices, and strive for an inclusive and empathetic approach in our scholarship and teaching.

Text Exemplar: *The Sharp Edge of Silence*

In this chapter, we use *The Sharp Edge of Silence* (Rosenblum, 2023) as a text exemplar to illustrate how C.A.R.E. can be used by teachers to avoid the troubling vignette at the opening of this manuscript. The voices of the girls in the novel were frequently silenced; the teachers were (initially) absent from the conversations; and there was not sufficient adult guidance or support for the students who experienced assault. Framing difficult discussions within a text rather than within students' experiences allows for discussions that may be able to engage in the nuance and complexity of an issue. This does not mean that a student is not allowed to bring in personal experience; it means that it is the student's choice as to whether that experience is shared. We chose this text because it provides a tool for discussion, and it provides a connection to Kat's lived experiences in the classroom discussion.

The Sharp Edge of Silence takes place at Lycroft Phelps, an exclusive boarding school, that provides students with both a top-quality education and access to the resources necessary to be successful at school and in life. *The Sharp Edge of Silence* is the story of a girl, Quinn, who returns to Lycroft Phelps the fall after she is raped by a fellow student who is protected from blame by school culture. The story is told from the point of view of three characters—Charlotte, Max, and Quinn—and the alternating first person narratives weave together to explore the aftermath of the assault. Charlotte, the perfect student riddled with self-doubt, and Max, the math genius quickly climbing to the top of the social ladder, provide counter perspectives to that of Quinn, the artistic dreamer who was raped. The novel delves into the complex issues of sexual violence, campus culture, secret societies, and the allure of team loyalty. The questions of what students will do to belong, to fit in, become central to the story. The role of silence as complicity threads through the narratives.

Caring for Students: A Framework of C.A.R.E.

The teacher in the opening example chose not to participate in the discussion at all; thus, we propose the following framework as a tool to begin addressing the challenging, emotionally fraught issues that require multiple levels of care from the teacher as an active participant in the planning of the discussion and in the discussion itself. Our framework for caring for students (drawing from Noddings, 2012) uses a developed acronym, C.A.R.E., that provides a structure for shaping instruction. This framework builds on Noddings (2012) ideas that to build strong, caring relationships, we have to include connections beyond school, validation of students' stories, critical responses, and willingness to try.

Facilitating discussions on difficult or challenging topics requires that educators think carefully about the tools and talk they will use with students. We have found that using a framework that grew out of our work with equity and relationship-focused pedagogies can provide guidance for how educators can develop a set of tools to engage with complex conversations. While selecting and using texts thoughtfully is important to achieving the goals established by the teacher, it is by itself insufficient. No text or even set of texts is adequate to engage students in thinking critically about the world without teachers also accounting for other pedagogical moves (e.g., the ways these texts are framed, how instruction engages with the topics, how learning is assessed). Further, educators must consider the context in which instruction is occurring and who is present in the classroom. By considering these aspects when planning and instructing, teachers can positively impact students' learning and attend to potential dangers in this work. To that end, we ask the questions, "What *else* needs to be considered when using YAL to have complex conversations with adolescents?" and "How do we move from text selection to text engagement as a way to show CARE *for* students?" In thinking about these questions in connection to texts that address rape, sexual assault, and rape culture, what else might we need to consider? For example, if there has been a recent sexual assault at the school, are there additional considerations that need to be made? What discussion preparations might need to be made in order to facilitate student participation? What activities might support student textual engagement while also supporting their emotional development?

In pursuing the aims of the C.A.R.E., framework with its focus on considering the analysis of the systems that create or replicate inequities, allows us to look at what silences both survivors and those who could speak up; the issues raised in the YA novels about rape, sexual assault, and rape culture are situated with larger contexts that mirror the contexts in which adolescents live. In addition to this stance, we consider this work within notions of critical care. In this sense, we encourage teachers who approach these topics to act with care – for the communities represented in the texts, for their students, and for themselves. That is, we ask teachers to be *care-ful*.

An Ethic of Care *for* Students

Noddings' concept of care, particularly as described in her works from 1992 and 2003, emphasizes a relational approach to caring. This approach contrasts the notions of "caring *for*" versus "caring *about*." Caring *about* allows the carer to act in a self-defined manner, based on their own sense of caring: *I* care *about* you. In contrast, caring *for*, according to Noddings, privileges the needs of the one cared for. It requires that the carer know something about the cared-for and possesses the skills to provide care in a particular way, not just inhabit a "caring" attitude. Noddings (1992) rejected paternalistic notions of "taking care of" someone else and called for teachers to care for their students in a way that is responsive to students' desires and that considers their physical, emotional, spiritual, and intellectual selves. Notably, she said, "Caring is a way of being in relation, not a set of specific behaviors" (p. 17). As a result, caring can only be said to happen when it leads to reception, recognition, and ultimately a reciprocal response from the one who is cared for. Selecting and using texts in a classroom cannot be boiled down to a checklist that teachers tick off, but instead, we ask teachers to *care-fully* consider how texts, students, families, communities, and they themselves might interact when engaged as part of a critical education curriculum.

For example, consider how the two educators in *The Sharp Edge of Silence* (Rosenblum, 2023) responded to Quinn's rape. Dean Frye attempts to force mediation arguing, "We need mediation to put this to rest. Did you tell her how it helps–how it makes the boy accountable to her" (p. 351) while Ms. Ballard counters with what Quinn has said she wants, saying, "She doesn't want to make anything of it…Just let her try to move on." (p. 377). Dean Frye pushes his notion of care by insisting on his solution. He says, "Look, what's done is done. We can't get it to un-happen. We just have to help her feel like she is being attended to…We need it to be resolved" (p. 377). Ms. Ballard has clearly listened to Quinn's expressed need while Dean Frye is focused on providing the "care" he has decided that Quinn needs. His care is patronizing and, ultimately, self-serving. It allows him to provide a solution that absolves him of further responsibility. Ms. Ballard realizes that more is needed and sets up supports for Quinn. These were supports that she discussed with Quinn first.

Drawing on Noddings (1992), caring for students is rooted in reciprocity, such that the carer understands how their caring affects others, and those receiving the care are able to care for themselves and show care for the carer. Hence, it's not enough to claim that simply reading *The Sharp Edge of Silence* shows care for students in our classrooms with experiences with sexual violence. We are also responsible for engaging with the text in a way that feels like caring to them and giving them space and time to care for themselves throughout the class's interaction with the text. In short, notions of critical care make it impossible to ignore the ethical implication of using any given text. Doing so, with attention solely on the text and not on our students, may lead to replicating the very forms of bias and inequity we are seeking to address by bringing the text into the curriculum. To operationalize this concept, educators can use the C.A.R.E. framework. This framework encourages teachers to:

- **Connect** with students on a personal level, understanding their unique needs and contexts
- **Amplify** the voices and experiences of students, ensuring they feel heard and valued
- **Recognize** the individuality of each student and the specific forms of support they require.
- **Embrace** a holistic approach to caring that considers students' physical, emotional, spiritual, and intellectual well-being.

By implementing this framework, educators can better align their practices with Noddings' relational and reciprocal model of care, fostering a more inclusive and responsive educational environment.

Connect the Text to the Students' Worlds. Showing CARE begins with providing opportunities for students to make explicit connections between the novel and their own lives in ways that critically analyze the role of systems of oppression. When we read a text that presents a challenging topic, part of our work beyond the novel is helping students see the full context. Quinn is a student struggling to heal from sexual assault; Max is a scholarship kid who is trying to navigate his conscious from the newfound popularity with the rowing team and secret society. Charlotte is questioning and trying to figure out her relationship with Seb based on his involvement in that same society. Quinn's nearly invisible experience at the dance and the aftermath of the assault is confusing and hard to talk about with her friends and as teachers with our students. We can ask students what else she, her experiences, and her classmates' struggles could represent in our lives? These three students represent different aspects of a system, which is designed to hide or silence a survivor. Max is a scholarship student trying to excel in his academic environment but, like any high school student, he also wants friends and relationships. How far will he go to belong? Charlotte is facing choices that are both personal—her romantic relationship—and community—her support of Quinn and other girls at the school—as she tries to negotiate what is right. Quinn is trying to figure out who she is in the aftermath; she wants to make choices for herself rather than have them made by someone else. These are experiences that students can connect with as readers.

When we ask students to **connect** the text with their own lived experiences and the sociopolitical realities of many of our students, we provide them with an opportunity to see that people do not experience things in the same way or always get the happy ending. We disrupt the 'single story' (Adichie, 2009). Moreover, we start to help them think about why that might be. It's important to remember, though, that when we encourage students to do this, they will bring that critical lens to our space -- and we have to be truly ready to hear what they want to tell us. Without this time to connect with the text we position the characters (and our students) as needing to "overcome the odds" in ways that suggest those who don't are failures.

Amplify the Voices of Those Represented. Once readers start to connect issues we're reading about with their own lives, they often have lots of stories to share or questions they want answered. This is an opportunity to educate students with the help of experts -- activists and lawyers, educational researchers, recovery counselors, mental health experts, and more. Bringing these folks in— or materials and resources offered by them to speak to the representations in the texts— helps students realize that the issues in stories extend beyond the novel. Validating others' voices and knowledge gives space to students who choose to narrate their related experiences or not and avoids tokenizing or outing them. These experiences are real, not just something we read about in a novel, but something that lives in our everyday world. Bringing in these perspectives provides the opportunity to constantly ask—"Why do we need people who work with rape survivors?" in ways that allow us to consider how the world we inhabit is constructed to ignore problems. And so, people who focus on breaking the status quo are often there to point out who has been left out and fight for their rights. We see in the text that Quinn does not begin to heal until she accepts help and support from people who are trained to work with survivors of rape and sexual assault. For example, Quinn confides in Ms. Ballard, a faculty member at the school with many titles, and Ms. Ballard offers Quinn several options to heal ranging from mediation to restorative justice protocols (Rosenblum, 2023, p. 342). Teachers and students can discuss the options from the text (and others) with the help of a trained professional. Students might create Public Service Announcements or posters to alert students about their options.

Recognize How Kids Come to Text. By thinking beyond single or simplified narratives of texts, we can anticipate some of possible ways students come to the text. In discussions with the students, we ask students to find parallels between different privileges and the benefits unfairly bestowed on different dominant groups. Readers learn about their own privileges, but also their complicities with injustice. We have to anticipate that readers may confront their own emotions, experiences, and behaviors. They may not have realized this was happening because such occurrences are normalized (i.e., "just the way things are"). For instance, in the text when Max begins to question whether he should go through with his initiation of retrieving Alex's underwear and join the secret boys' club. He has an internal dialogue, "What if I didn't follow through tonight? So what if I don't get the bunny ears. They're ridiculous. But then I think of the shit that will fly my way from Pearce, et al. And really, would I be here at all without the boys in the boat? If I don't seize the moment of my rise in status, I'll never get it back. And then Alex would lose interest" (Rosenblum, 2023, p. 425). Students can reflect on a time when their own conscience was in conflict and begin to consider how they negotiated with themselves the choices made and what they might do differently in the same scenario again.

Embrace the Risk. When discussing topics like rape and sexual assault with students, there are inherent risks that educators must navigate. These risks are twofold: the potential discomfort and emotional distress these conversations can cause, and the consequences of avoiding such topics altogether. First, addressing difficult topics like sexual violence can trigger intense emotional reactions among students, including trauma survivors. Educators need to be prepared to handle these responses sensitively and provide appropriate support. This involves creating a safe and supportive classroom environment where students feel comfortable expressing their feelings and thoughts. Teachers must also be trained to recognize signs of distress and know how to refer students to additional support services when necessary.

However, avoiding these conversations can also be risky. When we shy away from discussing rape and sexual assault, we miss the opportunity to challenge and deconstruct harmful societal norms and myths surrounding these issues. Silence perpetuates ignorance and allows damaging stereotypes and misconceptions to persist unchallenged. By engaging with these topics, educators can help students unlearn prejudiced views and gain a more nuanced understanding of consent, boundaries, and respect. Teaching such sensitive material requires educators to embrace the inherent risks with full awareness of the challenges. This means preparing thoroughly, anticipating potential difficulties, and being ready to navigate them constructively. It also involves being transparent about these challenges with students, fostering an environment where open and respectful dialogue is encouraged.

Engaging students in discussions about sexual violence can help dismantle the privileging of certain groups and expose the systemic inequalities that underpin societal norms. As Kumashiro (2000) suggests, educational approaches should aim to disrupt the status quo and make visible the processes that privilege certain identities while marginalizing others. Schools play a significant role in transmitting societal ideologies and reinforcing existing power structures. Challenging these structures is inherently risky but necessary for promoting social justice and equity.

Students should be made aware of how societal norms are constructed and how these norms regulate behavior and identity, often punishing those who deviate from them. Texts like *The Sharp Edge of Silence* (Rosenblum, 2023) provide a valuable tool for these discussions, offering a 'brave space' where students can explore complex issues surrounding rape culture and sexual assault. In this space, students can confront uncomfortable truths, question their assumptions, and develop a deeper understanding of these critical issues. In sum, while there are significant risks associated with teaching about rape and sexual assault, the risks of not addressing these topics are even greater.

Final Thoughts

Talking about rape and sexual assault is difficult and requires careful planning and attention to text and the students. Centering the discussions in texts provides an opportunity for teachers and students to discuss complex issues in ways that push against traditional constructions, allowing students to take a critical perspective. Using the CARE framework allows for the development of empathy and critical thinking around complicated topics. This framework centers the work that teachers must do on themselves as they center students in preparation to use a text that pushes on ways to provide support for thinking and questioning. The need for ongoing conversations in classrooms around this topic is clear. Consent, what it is, what it isn't, and how it can change is an important place to start. It is not, however, an easy place to start. Beres (2020) argued that "[w]hile the majority of educators considered that sexual consent education was central to prevention, the perception of what type of consent education would lead to sexual violence prevention varied" (p. 232). Thus, we must go beyond a simple, uncomplicated definition of consent to a fully realized complex understanding to make a real change.

While *The Sharp Edge of Silence* (Rosenblum, 2023) provides insight into how a fictional school and its students handle a rape, it holds a mirror up to the ways in which society treats survivors of rape and sexual assault. As demonstrated in the novel, the institution attempts to hide the survivor's pain, and allows the abuser to continue patterns of abuse. We encourage educators to use such texts to build nuanced perspectives and deeper understandings about sexual violence and rape culture. Educators must be prepared to navigate these challenges thoughtfully and with sensitivity, fostering an environment where difficult but necessary conversations can take place. By doing so, they empower students to think critically about societal norms and work towards a more just and equitable society.

References

Adams, B. (2020). "I didn't feel confident talking about this issue...but I knew I could talk about a book": Using young adult literature to make sense of #metoo. *Journal of Literacy Research, 52*(2) 209–230.

Adichie, C. N. (2009, July). *The danger of a single story* [Video]. TED Conferences. https://www.ted.com/talks/chimamanda_ngozi_adichie_the_danger_of_a_single_story?language=en

Alsup, J.(2015). *A case for teaching literature in the secondary school*. Taylor & Francis.

Anderson, L. H. (2011). *Speak*. Square Fish.

Arao, B., & Clemens, K. (2013). From safe spaces to brave spaces: A new way to frame dialogue around diversity and social justice. In L. M. Landreman (Ed.), *The art of effective facilitation* (pp. 135-150). Stylus Publishing, LLC.

Beres, M. (2020). Perspectives of rape-prevention educators on the role of consent in sexual violence prevention. *Sex Education, 20*(2), 227-238.

Colantonio-Yurko, K. C., Adams, B., Boehm, S., & Miller, H. C. (2023). Boundaries, objectification, and gender norms: Addressing sexual and gender-based harassment with middle grade literature. *Middle School Journal, 54*(1), 23-31.

Curwood, J. S. (2013). Redefining normal: A critical analysis of (dis)ability in young adult literature. *Children's Literature in Education, 44*, 15-28.

Gee, J. (2017). *Teaching, learning, literacy in our high-risk high-tech world: A framework for becoming human*. Teachers College Press.

Herb, A. (2021). (Para)normalizing rape culture: Possession as rape in young adult paranormal romance. *Girlhood Studies: An Interdisciplinary Journal, 14*(1), 68-85.

Kualdi, J. (2023, May 20). 32 Shocking Sexual Assault Statistics for 2023. *Legal Jobs*. https://legaljobs.io/blog/sexual-assault-statistics#:~:text=Rape%20Statistics%20show%20that%20less,something%20shameful%2C%20hence%20victim%20reluctance.

Kumashiro, K. (2004). Uncertain beginnings: Learning to teach paradoxically. *Theory into Practice, 43*(2), 111-115.

Malo-Juvera, V. (2014). Speak: The effect of literacy instruction on adolescents' rape myth acceptance. *Research in the Teaching of English, 48*(4), 407–427.

Moore, A. (2024). Representations of testimonial smothering and critical witnessing of rape victim-survivors in Laurie Halse Anderson's *Speak* fanfiction. *Children's Literature in Education, 55,* 162-178.

Noddings, N. (1992). *The challenge to care in schools: An alternative approach to education.* Teachers College Press.

Noddings, N. (2003). *Caring: A feminine approach to ethics and moral education* (2nd Ed.). University of California Press.

Noddings, N. (2012). The caring relation in teaching. *Oxford Review of Education, 38*(6), 771-781.

O'Neill, L. (2016). *Asking for it.* Quercus.

Peters, M., & Besley, T. (2019). Weinstein, sexual predation, and 'rape culture': Public pedagogies and Hashtag internet activism. *Educational Philosophy and Theory, 51*(5), 458-464.

Polletta, F., Chen, P. C. B., Gardner, B. G., & Motes, A. (2011). The sociology of storytelling. *Annual Review of Sociology, 37,* 109-130.

Rape, Abuse & Incest National Network. (n.d.). *Children and teen: Statistics.* https://www.rainn.org/statistics/children-and-teens

Righi, M. K., Bogen, K. W., Kuo, C., & Orchowski, L. M. (2021). A qualitative analysis of beliefs about sexual consent among high school students. *Journal of Interpersonal Violence, 36*(15-16), NP8290-NP8316.

Rosenblum, C. K. (2023). *The sharp edge of silence.* Quill Tree Books.

Storer, H. L., & Strohl, K. R. (2017). A primer for preventing teen dating violence? The representation of teen dating violence in young adult literature and its implications for prevention. *Violence Against Women, 23*(14), 1730–1751.

van den Toren, S. J., van Grieken, A., Lugtenberg, M., Boelens, M., & Raat, H. (2019). Adolescents' views on seeking help for emotional and behavioral problems: A focus group study. *International Journal of Environmental Research and Public Health, 17*(1), 191.

II. Critical Analysis of Youth Texts

"I want my entrance fee back": Institutional Betrayal in Young Adult Sexual Assault Narratives

Amber Moore, The University of British Columbia and
Elizabeth Marshall, Simon Fraser University

> Dr. Blasey Ford's experience is all too consistent with stories we heard and lived while attending Holton. Many of us are survivors ourselves. Holton's motto teaches students to "find a way or make one." We dream of making a world where women are free from harassment, assault, and sexual violence. We are deeply grateful to Dr. Blasey Ford for bravely stepping forward and bringing us closer to that world we all seek.
>
> -Open letter from 1984 Holton Alumnae https://www.standwithblaseyford.com/

In 2018, the world watched as Dr. Christine Blasey Ford spoke out against Supreme Court nominee, Brett Kavanaugh, about being sexually assaulted by him when they both attended Holton-Arms School. As this paper's opening epigraph addresses, Dr. Ford's experience of rape culture at this boarding school was not unique; rather, the open letter — signed by 1,234 Holton alumnae — discusses how many students became victim-survivors, left to "find a way" through violence without institutional support. Brett Kavanaugh went on to be appointed to a lifetime position in the most powerful court in the United States and at the time of this writing, has most recently used this role to help revoke 50 years of American feminist progress regarding reproductive rights by reversing Roe vs. Wade.

With this backdrop of the "rareified world" (Gaztambide-Fernández, 2009) wherein adolescence and violence(s) often collide, this paper examines young adult (YA) sexual assault narratives set in elite boarding schools similar to Holton, which Dr. Blasey Ford attended. We analyze YA novels, including *Honor Code* (Burkhart, 2018), *The Mockingbirds* (Whitney, 2010), and *Tradition* (Kiely, 2018) with an attention to how rape culture(s) manifest in the particular elite spaces and places of boarding schools in these texts. Moore (2018) has previously argued that it is important to attend to where sexual violence in YA literature takes place, asserting that the space and place of rape often serve as accomplices to rapists. Indeed, in these texts, the violence of rape extends beyond the perpetrators to be compounded by the site of sexual trauma and its consequent fallout:

at the schools themselves. We argue that the schools in these novels are sites of "institutional betrayal," a term referring to how institutions fail or harm dependent members by failing to act or by practicing overt discrimination (Parnitzke Smith & Freyd, 2014). Institutional betrayal in these elite boarding narratives take on three forms that include: (1) protecting policies congruent with rape cultures, the place of the school by way of physical appearance to maintain optics, as well as perpetrators, (2) prioritizing capitalism and control over consent culture by way of legacies and reputation, and (3) by outsourcing care and justice work to students.

At this juncture, it is also important to situate ourselves in this project and offer insight into what brings us to this work, as well as how our positionalities and politics inform it. We share a number of subject positions as able-bodied, cis, straight white women in academia who endeavor to engage in feminism that attends to intersectionality in our teaching, research, and personal lives. Both individually and in collaboration (with one another as well as other scholars), we have dedicated much scholarly attention to children's and YA literatures and popular culture texts that explore violence(s), particularly sexual violence, as this is an insidious feminist issue that we have each long been invested in resisting. As such, this chapter marks another effort to find new critical lenses for analysis of rape culture and representations of it, especially how it impacts youth culture(s).

Rape Culture, Boarding Schools, and the School Story
Rape Culture

Just as rape culture has long existed, it has unfortunately also been ever-present in schools. Much research has captured the ways in which sexual violence has permeated educational institutions of all levels, from K-12 to postsecondary. For example, in Buchwald, Fletcher, and Roth's early and groundbreaking book, *Transforming a Rape Culture*, Stein suggests that K-12 schools are typically "training grounds" (p. 58) for domestic and sexual violence as sexual abuse and harassment are "pervasive" (p. 65). This insidiousness continues into post-secondary – indeed, Dr. Ford's experience discussed in the introduction is an example that exploded into public discourse in 2018 and a plethora of research has interrogated campus rape culture, including so-called safety programs that typically reify rape myths and perpetuate further harm. For instance, Hall (2004) has significantly argued that post-secondary campus safety pedagogies for rape prevention function to encourage women's treatment as potential "rape spaces" (p. 2).

More recently, work on rape culture in schools has been done to address the ways in which rape culture is increasingly manifesting online and disrupting the education experiences of learners; for example, Ringrose et al. (2022) examine online sexual harassment, cyberflashing, and image based-sexual abuse impacting young people across K-12 schools in England, which is indicative of how rape cultures continue to evolve across a number of Western educational contexts. As such, rape remains ever-present in school spaces of all kinds, including elite one. Next, we turn to particular considerations worth keeping in mind with respect to boarding schools as cultures, communities, and institutions and the ways in which these spaces can especially be sites for harm and trauma.

Boarding Schools

Boarding schools are a particular form of schooling wherein typically wealthy children are sent to elite, intensive schools to learn and live; they are especially popular in Australia, Europe, and North America and are generally designed to immerse young students in academic life for the purposes of achieving better scholastic outcomes (Raiker, 2024). Schools promise such outcomes by offering smaller class sizes, increased access to educators, exceptional experiential learning opportunities, as well as dynamic and exclusive extra-curricular opportunities (Behegahel et al., 2017). It is important to note that we distinguish boarding schools from how we define other sorts of specialized schools such as (1) day schools — private schools for daily education where learners live with their families and not on school campus, (2) for-profit so-called "troubled teen" industry programs (e.g. therapeutic boarding schools such as "last chance" ranches), as well as (3) residential schools (sometimes referred to as boarding schools).

The boarding schools in the texts under examination in this paper are the exclusive domain of members of a new elite with considerable capital and power passed through families with only some exceptions, as demonstrated by a couple of YA characters under discussion here who are admitted on through scholarship programs. While research on boarding schools is generally lacking (Martin et al., 2014), numerous studies document negative experiences in them, including trauma (e.g. see Duffet & Bassett, 2016; Jack, 2020; Simpson, 2018) — even sexual trauma, and so much so that "boarding school syndrome" (Schaverien, 2015) exists. In short, boarding schools are understood here as educational spaces and places characterized by long legacies of excellence that foster a collective identity among students and alumni, formal rules, schedules and regulations, manicured grounds, strict philosophies and policies, and incredible wealth.

The School Story

As described by Musgrave (2016), the school story — in particular, the Western-centric boys' school story, emerged in the mid-nineteenth century, flourished, and then quickly fell out of popularity. The first full-length children's book is a girls' boarding school story, *The Governess; or, The Little Female Academy* (Fielding, 1749) and an oft-cited example of this genre is *Tom Brown's Schooldays* (Hughes, 1857). School stories are a particular version of a bildungsroman (that is, a coming-of-age story focused on character growth), largely characterized by imperialism, homoeroticism, and whiteness (Reimer, 2009); after all, "the politics of space and place organize students' ideas experiences in ways that highlight how broader social dynamics of race, class, gender, and sexuality interact with geography, even in elite spaces" (Gaztambide-Fernández, 2009). School stories typically include a secondary school setting and are written from the perspectives of usually middle-class children because at the height of these stories' popularity, children of low socioeconomic status were rarely sent to school (Clark, 1996).

However, the genre has increasingly grown diverse, as a range of dynamic YA texts take place in boarding schools. For example, the *Harry Potter* series (Rowling, 1997-2007) is usually considered part of the school story tradition (see Duggan, 2017; Fowler, 2019; Mynott, 1999). The innovative queer-romance and science fiction graphic novel *On a Sunbeam* (Walden, 2018) includes queer and nonbinary characters and is set at a boarding school in space. Other YA texts continue to use the school site as a space for innovative stories such as the horror story *Wilder Girls* (Power, 2019), the mystery *Looking for Alaska* (Green, 2006), and the dystopian narrative *Maggot Moon* (Gardner & Crouch, 2013), just to name a few. These dynamic fresh takes on the school story demonstrate how the genre is being necessarily expanded to include characters with complex intersectional identities and who have unique embodied and lived experiences. As such, there is ongoing interest in school stories (see, for example, Epic Reads, n.d.; Gutman, 2019; Marshall, 2016; 2018; 2020; Ryland, 2022) and indeed because "the school story continues to thrive while crossing mediums, audiences, and cultures," it is therefore a "classic" genre with "contemporary significance" (Aitchison, 2022, p. 9), which we certainly find evidence of in the texts under examination here, as these school stories are placed in particular rape cultures, therefore reshaping the genre as well as offering necessary critiques of boarding schools in particular.

Conceptual Framework: Institutional Betrayal

We analyze rape culture in YA boarding school novels through the theoretical lens of institutional betrayal. Institutional betrayal (Parnitzke Smith & Freyd, 2013; 2014) is informed by betrayal trauma theory (Freyd, 1997) and cultural betrayal trauma theory (e.g., Gómez & Freyd, 2018; Gómez, 2022), and takes place when powerful institutions perpetuate and/or compound harm experienced by people within those institutions who are dependent on them for care, guidance, safety, and wellbeing. In this way, institutional betrayal focuses on how people are bound to and by the systems and policies of institutions. A particularly damning quality of institutional betrayal is that it often operates insidiously and invisibly, sometimes without the knowledge of those who are being directly impacted by it; this means that it is all the more difficult and less likely for communities within institutions to organize against them and/or foster support systems. Institutional betrayal can happen in companies, governments, hospitals and care centers, militaries, religious institutions, and schools. As such, it has broad applications across many places and spaces as well as types of injustice and violence, but especially with respect to the issue of legacies of rape culture(s) in schools. It is worth noting that the sites where institutional betrayal often happens are places where safety should be paramount and particular ethics of care are expected to be in operation; vulnerable populations such as children, disabled, elderly, ill, and traumatized people largely frequent places such as care homes, hospitals, schools, treatment centers, and religious institutions, for example. Further, as Duffy et al. (2023) assert in their research on affects of workplace institutional betrayal and sexual harassment, institutional betrayal often manifests in neoliberal organizations and typically disadvantage historically marginalized and racialized groups while affording more opportunities to straight white men. While they discuss places of employment and not schools, it informs an understanding that institutional betrayal might not impact white male students as it does other learners.

Much like Dr. Christine Blasey Ford, many other victim-survivors have spoken out about similar experiences of rape culture in elite boarding schools. Real-world example of institutional betrayal that add a cultural backdrop to the YA novels under examination for this paper and include memoirs like *I Have a Right To* (Prout & Abelson, 2018), which examines how Prout was raped by a fellow student, testified against him, and stood up to public backlash. Another is *Notes on a Silencing* (Crawford, 2020), which describes how, after two male peers assaulted Crawford, she was refused institutional support and was further silenced. Each text tackles how these women were both attacked at St. Paul's boarding school in New Hampshire. Crawford has continued to speak out about the institutional betrayal committed by their former boarding school that, according to these accounts, knowingly perpetuates sexual violence. To quote St. Paul's current school safety commitments as stipulated on their website at the time of this writing, they have "a zero-tolerance policy for conduct that is at odds with our commitment to providing a safe and welcoming environment for everyone in our community to live, learn, and work" ("School safety"). They also now have a page dedicated to "legacy abuse" for alumni who experienced sexual violence during schooling. This is in keeping with more recent trends to show a willingness to demonstrate awareness of institutional wrongdoing, engage in betrayal reparation practices (Parnitzke Smith & Freyd, 2013; 2014), and move towards institutionally courageous work. What the texts under examination in this paper offer are literary insights regarding how institutional betrayal can compound adolescents' experiences with rape cultures that nested within the particular context of a boarding school. These stories function together to make clear the need for rigorous institutional courage, especially when it comes to places and spaces for young people and their education.

Boarding School Betrayal: Rape Culture Across Three YA Texts

All three YA texts analyzed here are contemporary versions of the school story that speak to contemporary concerns regarding rampant rape culture through confrontations of the reality of juvenile offenders — a truth often ignored (Manne, 2020), even as we are in the midst of this MeToo era. It is important to note that whiteness is pervasive across all of these stories which aligns with racial demographics typical in many Western boarding schools (e.g., see Brown, 2016; see also Ayling, 2019 for an examination of whiteness as a marketing tactic). Please note that all protagonists and the majority of characters across these texts are described or depicted as white. For example, the book cover art of editions of both *The Mockingbirds* and *Tradition* include white people and in *Honor Code*, the character Harper remarks at one point: "Rich white kids assaulting each other at their fancy private boarding school? You don't want to get in the middle of that kind of thing" (p. 146). Like boarding school stories, YA sexual assault narratives have a problem with whiteness (Hubler, 2017) with exceptions slowly increasing in the genre. As such, this small sample of texts that merge both genres demonstrate a lack of diversity that needs to continue to shift as YA literature needs to better attend to representing dynamic intersectional experiences of victim-survivors.

Honor Code tells the complicated story of Sam who is grateful to be attending Edwards Academy to help fulfill her Ivy League dreams; however, when she claims she has been sexually violated, she seeks justice by speaking out via blogging and contacting a journalist. The story's major twist is that Sam managed to escape her would-be attacker and she pretends to be a victim-survivor when it is her friend, Gracie, who experienced the testimony she tells. Indeed, this story demonstrates how institutional betrayal "is associated with complex outcomes similar to those associated with interpersonal betrayal" (Parnitzke Smith & Freyd, 2014, p. 578) as Gracie experiences both institutional betrayal by her school that she ultimately leaves, as well as by Sam who steals her story and experience. Next, *The Mockingbirds* centers on Alex, who wakes up one morning at Themis Academy in the bed of a classmate she doesn't remember having sex with. Finally relenting to the urging of her sister and friends who help her to understand that she's been raped, she seeks help from the school's secret society that fights for justice, The Mockingbirds, who put her rapist on trial for his crime. As such, while this story focuses on one victim-survivor, this story especially emphasizes the power of community responses to rape culture. Finally, *Tradition* alternates perspectives with each new chapter, following two students: newcomer scholarship student James (Jamie) and Jules, a known rebel at their school, Fullbrook Academy. When a former boyfriend assaults Jules and a fellow victim-survivor classmate is harassed and slut-shamed, Jules and Jamie form a bond to resist their local rape culture; once again, this story emphasizes on the necessity for collective action against rape culture and how critical and creative social justice can be enacted to combat violence.

Across *Honor Code*, *The Mockingbirds*, and *Tradition*, institutional betrayal runs rampant, especially presenting as (1) protecting policies congruent with rape cultures, the place of the school by way of physical appearance to maintain optics, as well as perpetrators, (2) prioritizing capitalism and control over consent culture by way of legacies and reputation, and (3) by outsourcing care and justice work to students. All these qualities collectively lead to sending significant messages to students that they are not the primary concern of school leaders, resulting in either blatant institutional betrayal or students' anticipation and/or perceptions of institutional betrayal, keeping students quiet about violence— at least within their schools. These messages are especially damning considering the ways in which these educative places and spaces are also homes to these students, and therefore arguably demand a higher standard of ethic of care by the schools to foster safe environments at the very least, as well as demonstrate the necessity for institutional courage when that safety is threatened in any way.

Protecting Place, Policies & Perpetrators

One of the first ways in which institutional betrayal manifests in these texts is how the schools prioritize prestige by protecting the actual place of the exquisite and exclusive campuses, the policies that run them, and the perpetrators who run rampant in them. This is to say that the fictional schools in these YA texts focus on optics to emphasize their comprehensive organization which is especially evidenced by the manicured and regal grounds of the campuses, the creation of strict codes of conduct for the students who inhabit these spaces, and practicing neglect with respect to the terrible behavior of many of their privileged students including perpetrators, to keep up appearances.

To begin with, leaders of the fictional boarding schools, Edwards, Fullbrook, and Themis, all promote perceptions and reputations of excellence by presenting exceptionally pleasing places — that is, emphasizing "'maintaining appearances' at all costs" (Parnitzke Smith & Freyd, 2014, p. 580). Each novel includes discussions and descriptions of luxurious and luring locations: physical campuses that maintain veneers—visual messages of prestige—indeed, a quality of institutional betrayal. *Honor Code*'s campus is a distraction for the intense lifestyle it demands including hazing traditions; Sam reflects that instead of feeling humiliated, she "focused on how beautiful the campus is, drenched in the early morning sunlight" (Burkhart, 2018, p. 19). Before Sam realizes the rape culture permeating Edwards, she is anxious to return while visiting home, thinking: "I can't wait to get back to the Edwards world of huge old trees and fantastical brick buildings" (p. 62).

Similarly, students in *Tradition* are constantly aware of Fullbrook's awesomeness; Jamie marvels that "even the watery reflections in the stained-glass windows seemed curated, cultivated, perfected. History was everywhere" (Kiely, 2018, p. 11). This perfection is such a fixture that Jamie even notices when leaves litter the walkways, musing that the maintenance crew likely had the day off or were perhaps rebelling, refusing to keep up the ongoing place-making activity of projecting its vision of being manicured and well-mannered. Because Jamie is a working-class scholarship student, he sees past Fullbrook's gloss and understands the incredible labor required to maintain its appearance. *The Mockingbirds* also emphasizes the campus' beauty — its "old brick structures, Victorian buildings, and Colonial-style mansions converted into halls of learning" (Whitney, 2010, p. 13). However, it is noteworthy that it is not as apparent in this text, which might be because unlike Sam and Jamie who are on scholarship, Alex is a more typically wealthy pupil — in fact, she is a legacy student, with an older sister having attended as well — and as such, might not take much notice.

Returning to *Tradition*, perhaps this is why when Jules, Jamie, and friend Aileen riot against Fullbrook's rape culture, they take aim at its optics by burning "No" — a "fiery tattoo" (Kiely, 2018, p. 328) into the grass of an athletic field, forcing the once-pleasing space to become one of protest. Thus, the campus serves a dual purpose of making the school look prestigious but also distracting from its uglier issues — namely, rape culture and the accompanying institutional betrayal. After all, institutions regularly point to prestige as a way of assuaging any doubts about harm possibly happening there (Parnitzke Smith & Freyd, 2013; 2014). The impressive physicality of the campuses then all similarly function as powerful measures for institutional self-protection; in maintaining picture-perfect veneers, the schools are able to convey a pleasing sense of grandeur, order, and indeed, care. The carefully tended to spaces and places of these schools offer a veil of safety and security in their beauty, exclusivity, and close upkeep so that they are understood as ideal homes for students.

All three fictional boarding schools also enforce strict policies for their students through codes of conduct, relying on these documents to maintain order.

Lind et. al. (2020) describe how high schools might enact institutional courage to be supportive of students as they navigate issues such as gender harassment, and developing transparent policies that comply with criminal laws and civil codes is considered necessary. Institutional courage (Center for Institutional Courage, n.d.) is an antidote to institutional betrayal wherein an institution endeavors to be accountable and transparent following wrongdoings and protect those they are responsible for. For example, Freyd asserts that "Sincere institutional apologies for institutional betrayal are an important step in the institutional-courage direction" (n.d.) and suggests a number of general principles that institutions can enact. Examples include self-study for internal monitoring, educating institutional leaders on trauma such as sexual violence, and activating an institution's power to contribute to social change.

Yet, the policies of these boarding schools cannot be described in such a way. As a result, students are well aware of the expectations and boundaries regarding their behavior but they are unclear about how the school will keep them safe. Further, they are not only expected to follow the explicit policies, but they must also be mindful of the cloudier, implicated instructions as well; as Sam in *Honor Code* describes:

> living by the rules means living by *their* rules. It means molding yourself into the thing they want you to be and then keeping yourself like that, posed and squashed and strangled until you no longer remember what you once looked like, acted like, or thought like. (Burkhart, 2018, p. 91)

She goes on to point out the slipperiness of the code — so important that it is indeed the title of the book, yet so ineffective; students only obey "until they don't want to anymore" (p. 121). The code is upheld in surprising ways, trumping other systems including the police, with Sam noting that "Going to the cops would be breaking the honor code in a huge way" (p. 148).

If the code is meant to protect students to such an extent that it supersedes the police, then Edwards is committing a particularly insidious form of institutional betrayal by isolating students rather than being congruent with other governing bodies. Sam goes as far as calling the code "cultish," accusing that it "created a self-regulating community" that might "piss off" "a lot of wealthy, white people if it were exposed" (p. 151). A fellow victim-survivor at Edwards named Olivia tells Sam that the code was actually the reason why she didn't disclose her trauma — that in fact, she was scared to come forward because offering testimony about sexual assault would *break* the code. This is in stark contrast to what an institutionally courageous school should do if their students experience rape culture: sensitively respond to disclosures (sharing sexual trauma testimony) (Lind et al. 2020).

In *Tradition*, Fullbrook's motto is "ready to take on the world" (Kiely, 2018, p. 13) - indeed, very capitalist and imperialist in spirit. However, it is revealed that the "unspoken" motto understood by students is "This is how to grow up — eat shit and learn how to smile" (p. 203). In *The Mockingbirds*, the code of conduct has a similarly powerful presence and yet it carries no substance; Alex scoffs: "Code of conduct?" then bites her tongue, thinking: "I don't say what I really want to say — their code of conduct means nothing. There is only one code of conduct that matters here at Themis" (Whitney, 2010, p. 244). These policies then function as kinds of invisible fences that cause considerable damage; even as the schools claim to hold rigid rules to keep students out of harm's way, they produce many frustrated and frightened students who seek escape.

Finally, the leaders of these institutions practice neglect with respect to rape culture such as ignoring the terrible behavior of many of their privileged students, including perpetrators. Returning to *Honor Code's* Edwards Academy, it is immediately revealed that it has a reputation for trouble — a "patchy background" (Burkhart, 2018, p. 4). Later, more directly, Sam writes on her blog:

> Boarding school looks like: knowing there are a lot of fucked up things hiding under the surface of your school. But not realizing just how fucked up it is until its too late. (p. 123)

Tearing, Sam's friend and victim-survivor Gracie offers a hard truth about their school's thriving culture of permissiveness: "This is Edwards Academy, Sam. You aren't supposed to know. And everyone lets [the rapist] get away with it" (p. 133). This is an example of how students' perceptions of institutional betrayal can lead to severe consequences for their wellbeing. Their teacher, Mrs. Barker, even agrees with the girls in speaking to a reporter, revealing that although parents trust the school to keep their children safe, "the enemy" is "inside the school itself" (p. 201). Boarding schools, in combining home, leisure, and work for children, are institutions that "foster a sense of trust *or* dependency from their members (often both)" (Parnitzke Smith & Freyd, 2014, p. 578). And yet, because the rapist in this text is a well-known predator with students tracking his violence from junior high to high school, it is likely that at some (or many) points, adults were also made aware of his violence. As such, it is likely that Edwards maintains a pattern of "not knowing" making it a school where, potentially, "abuse is "common knowledge" but unaddressed" (Parnitzke Smith & Freyd, 2014, p. 581).

In *The Mockingbirds*, a moment of despair for Alex unfolds when school administrators are angered by the decision for Shakespeare's *The Tempest* (which includes a scene of rape) to be acted out in class between Alex and her harasser. As the principal assures, "We don't want to create a climate where it seems we're condoning rape," Alex wants to scream: "But you do and you have [...] You created this, you created this place, this perception, this environment" (Whitney, 2010, p. 246). Alex is harassed several times throughout the novel by her rapist and his friends, such as when he calls her to accuse her of being a "delusional" (p. 214) "freak girl" (p. 215). This is all evidence of how her school fails to take proactive steps to prevent such a "climate."

Jules in *Tradition* also deals with much similar harassment, from male peers commenting on her body to being called a "feminazi" (Kiely, 2018, p. 214), and, like Alex, having her attacker diminish his violence with, "I didn't rape you, Jules. Don't blow this all out of proportion" (p. 215). However, the school ignores the ongoing harassment, compounding trauma; for example, Jules reveals that there's "Only one adult [she] could really trust" (p. 238) and even in going to her, this person seems distracted during their talk. Even further, it seems that some adults do further damage by actually buoying the bad behavior of some students, including perpetrators. For example, in *Honor Code*, a group of boys including the rapist are allowed to smoke and drink on campus by the provost, sending the message that they can act as they please, creating an environment where violence is more likely to occur. This culture of permissiveness and hidden curriculum is an instance demonstrating how boarding schools are places where the beginnings of better lives for a chosen few are fostered; graduates like these characters might one day have access to significant social networks comprised of faculty and fellow peers, endowing them to continue this tradition of protected misbehavior as they move on to other elite institutions such as universities and workplaces.

Capitalism and Control vs. Consent

Another way in which institutional betrayal manifests in these texts is through these schools' decisions to prioritize capitalism and control over cultivating a culture of consent. The failure to prevent abuse is a quality of institutional betrayal, which is certainly ongoing across these texts as school legacies and reputation are of the utmost importance, upheld through thriving cultures of gatekeeping, control, and silence. To begin with, neither Sam in *Honor Code* nor Jamie in *Tradition* are "typical" rich boarding school kids; Sam begged her parents to take on this "Titanic of expenditures" (Burkhart, 2018, p. 3) while Jamie earned a scholarship spot as an athlete. At one point, Sam even laments, "I want my entrance fee back" (p. 123). As such, both are very aware of their schools' gatekeeping; Sam wonders if she will make it to her second year and Jamie has near-constant anxiety about being an invited guest. His first clear thought at Fullbrook is "*I do not belong here*. I didn't have the right clothes, the right hairstyle, the right way to speak" (Kiely, 2018, p. 9). His feelings are not just personal worries either; Jules' attacker says to him, "you don't understand anything about Fullbrook. You don't belong here, dude" before instructing, "go back to whatever dirty little garage you crawled out of" (p. 279) and threatening, "I can ruin you […] I can sue your ass and sue your family and bankrupt that shitty little hardware store back in Bumfuck Nowhere and ruin you and everyone" (p. 281).

As such, Sam and Jamie both suffer under the capitalist ideas and practices that the school embraces including but not limited to supporting private wealth accumulation that excludes others (e.g. high tuition), emphasizing productivity as a measure of worthiness, thereby perpetuating the myth of exceptionalism (e.g. high and narrow assessment standards), and encouraging students to feel as though we either succeed or fail on our own. As a result, both characters feel precarious at school, at risk of having to leave at any time, and without trusted adults to help alleviate their worries or navigate these spaces. Due to these feelings, when Sam is faced with and Jamie witnesses rape culture, their precariousness intensifies. For example, Sam considers how leveraging her violent experience might help ease feeling like an outsider, self-chastising with: "I should be happy that the hottest, smartest, coolest guy possible picked me. I could tell anyone we did it last night, and I'd suddenly be Scully's girlfriend. I'd be in the club" (p. 123).

Boarding school stories are usually exclusively white (Fowler, 2019), demonstrating how capitalism and white supremacy intersect. Like boarding school stories, whiteness is pervasive in many YA sexual assault narratives with exceptions slowly increasing in the genre. Of these novels, *Tradition* pays some attention to racist gatekeeping. For example, Jamie remarks to Jules: "Fullbrook is super white" (Kiely, 2018, p. 101) to which Jules responds, "It's a problem. Javi and I tried to get a Black Lives Matter vigil going last year." She reveals that it was ultimately unsuccessful; "This place is *way* too white for that." As such, it is likely that institutional betrayal of young people of color likely often happens at Fullbrook and many others are never able to access this school at all.

This issue of gatekeeping is part of and connected to the ways in which all the schools maintain cultures of control. Sam studies feverishly but is also resentful about how the school micromanages students, revealing: "I actually find Twilight Study Hour and Sunday Study kind of humiliating — like I can't be trusted to manage my own time" (Burkhart, 2018, p. 57). This is evidence of the school's distrust of students to be agentic as well as of their refusal to seek out student feedback, even at such a seemingly benign level. Instead, an intense sense of competition is fostered, denying students the ability to truly be and/or discover themselves. Sam charges:

> It is impossible to be yourself with anyone in this place. Like making a friend in prison- what you feel isn't real. It's just dependency. Survival. At some point the school is bound to get between you. All the head games, all the conformity, all this mindless dedication to the rules. (p. 91)

A strategy of maintaining control through this intense atmosphere is modeling and enabling hierarchies; as one student spats about another in *Honor Code*, "She's just a fucking Firstie" (p. 99).

This is evidence of the time-honored tradition across many schools to demean and dismiss beginning students as they transition from one school to another. These transition times can turn into experiences of much domination, coercion, and hazing by upper-level learners. Hazing — that is, abuse such as bullying, humiliation, intimidation, pranks, ridicule, and other destructive behaviors experienced by new and prospective students, figures prominently at the beginning of both Jules' and Sam's boarding school experiences. Jules actually intervenes in hazing to spare a first-year student from having to simulate oral sex on a banana by doing it herself and Sam, along with a group of new girls, are forced to strip down and have their bodies inspected and critiqued by fatphobic upper year girls who advise them on diet and exercise thereafter. Among other insults, Sam is told she has a "saggy" (p. 14) chest and feels deeply shamed. Sam notes the damage of these established hierarchies that rest on such experiences of hazing drives wedges between students, keeping them isolated and stressed; after fighting with her roommate, she reflects, "Edwards has gotten inside us. Acting like everything is okay, when we're really stretched like taffy so far that we're about to split in the middle" (p. 134).

It seems this hazing and these hierarchies are traditions and yet, the school does not address it, therefore normalizing abusive contexts. Rather, they thrive on these power systems where students largely police themselves and faculty only pick up in small but significant ways. For example, Jules argues with a sexist teacher because she has her tampon out on her desk instead of tucked away. This is indicative of the culture of control that thrives at Fullbrook, as well as the sexist atmosphere that informs its rape culture.

Another way in which school legacies and reputation are prioritized over interrogating and eradicating these schools' rape culture is through silencing practices that make it difficult to report difficult and/or violent experiences; as Sam says, "What happens in boarding school… stays in boarding school" (Burkhart, 2018, p. 44). This is why the blog in *Honor Code* is so significant; it represents an intimate revealing: a digital and public diary of what actually happens at Edwards even as Sam acknowledges halfway through her first year that she needs to "[stay] quiet and still, thinking that would help" (p. 120). Jules also learns that staying quiet is a strategy for self-preservation at Themis, returning to the mantra "One more year" throughout the book, which she says to herself over and over. She also stays silent to maintain scholastic success, learning that "it was better to fake it than to keep showing your ignorance" (Kiely, 2018, p. 79). When Jules' friend Aileen decides to wear the dress she was raped in to the school hockey game as a protest, the culture of silence is again evident as people turned away, refusing to look at her. However, as Jules put it, "Nobody at Fullbrook might have wanted to talk about it, but they couldn't deny seeing it" (p. 308). Aileen's resistance to the silence around Fullbrook's rape culture is in keeping with feminist activism of wearing and/or carrying where and what you were raped in; for example, Emma Sulkowitcz's "Carry That Weight" project and "What Were You Wearing?" exhibits. It is worth mentioning that Sam in *Honor Code* also wears the clothes she was attacked in for days. In *The Mockingbirds*, Alex's sister reveals that a student killed herself the year before she started and rather than honoring the student's memory and/or creating change to address mental health challenges among youth, "It was all sort of hush-hush" (Whitney, 2010, p. 93). Silencing is indeed a key component of the attitudes of leaders across all texts under examination.

Outsourcing Care & Justice Work

Finally, institutional betrayal surfaces in these three boarding school stories in the ways that the students are forced to offer care and justice work for and with one another because school leaders do not provide this labor. This presents in the ways that older students often pick up the slack in both formal and informal manners, functioning as mentors, parental and/or policing figures for younger students and one another. This outsourcing of care and justice works emphasizes how schools are marked by drastic age and power differences between staff and students, leading to abuse of this power via neglect.

To begin with, unfortunately, sometimes the demands for students to be caregivers is beyond their capacities, leading to how even as they endeavor to provide helpful guidance, their inexperienced "advice" compounds harm. For example, in *Honor Code*, alongside the hazing that takes place, a significant amount of women's safety pedagogical work (Hall, 2004) is enacted. Edwards girls feel that they must keep one another safe because the adults won't. Edwards girls are given a list of good and bad boys: those who are safe and not. Because potential and established predator students at their schools are left unchecked, girls are left to look out for one another, and often reinforce damaging rape scripts and myths as they do so. For example, one girl instructs the newcomers: "Don't complain to us later if you go out with a 'naughty' guy and it doesn't go the way you want" (Burkhart, 2018, p. 11). Older students are known as dormitory or house "Moms" and "Dads," placing a huge burden on these young people to parent one another, leading to problems. This is exemplified by how confiding about sexual trauma to Sam's "House Mom" is immediately dismissed as a viable option because "then the whole school finds out" and her life at Edwards "is basically over" (p. 123). As well, her rapist's "House Dad" disregards fraternizing rules, ignoring Sam's presence in the boys' dorm, even when the bedroom door is closed — a clear policy violation. Sam muses, "Maybe he knew exactly what was going to happen that night. Maybe he let it happen" (p. 133).

With *Tradition*, in trying to spin the Fullbrook dynamic and its institutional betrayal of neglecting care as some sort of community and resiliency building project, Headmaster Patterson says in a speech to the student body: "People say you raise yourselves when you attend a school like ours, or better, that you raise each other [...] Do that as students have been doing here since 1801, raising themselves, raising each other" (Kiely, 2018, p. 53). This task — which could be easily characterized as an example of how institutional betrayal often goes undetected — is massive and taxing; as Jules describes, "It took a certain kind of strength to navigate Fullbrook mostly on her own all these years" (p. 88). However, students clearly struggle, like how Jamie breaks down in the arena, alone and sobbing, with only the echoes of his cries keeping him company, which he found "weirdly comforting" in a small way because it was "as if there was one other person crying along with [him]" (Kiely, 2018, p. 256).

Similarly in *The Mockingbirds*, as one character warns, "You have to watch your back because the teachers and administration won't do it for you" (Whitney, 2010, p. 80). Even further, it is known among students that Themis faculty allow all sorts of things to go on, "ignor[ing] everything because the very idea of bullying destroys their notion of who Themis students are — of who they're educating to be future leaders of the world and all that stuff" (p. 81). It is also mused that the faculty are in denial, assuming that "because Themis is this liberal, progressive school, nothing bad could happen here. There's no hate speech, no bullying here. How could there be?" (p. 93). Even if faculty did notice and acknowledge the ongoing issues at Themis such as its rape culture, "Teachers have no power" (176); rather, wealthy parents with "generations-deep allegiances" (Parnitzke Smith & Freyd, 2014, p. 575) and administration are the one who control the capital and culture.

The Mockingbirds holds one of the more damning examples of this dynamic of outsourced care work. Because Themis leaders never hold students accountable, a group of "masked avengers" (p. 98) students founded a secret society for "underground justice" (Whitney, 2010, p. 97) wherein they investigate and prosecute bad behavior; as a Mockingbird member named Martin puts it, "the school has given us no choice but to police ourselves" (p. 94). Unfortunately, this labor is necessary because "There are always too many cases. There's always someone doing something wrong" (p. 97). The Mockingbirds go on to support Alex through her rape accusation against Carver, bring him to trial and find him guilty. During the trial preparation, Mockingbird members act as allies, offering concrete support and comforting communication (DeTurk, 2011) to Alex such as ensuring she is accompanied across campus and debriefing with her.

Unlike the activist spirit apparent in many Mockingbirds, Jules is not as fortunate at Fullbrook. Though there are likely other students as concerned with justice as she is, she is left to do activist work alone. For example, her story opens with Jules standing on campus, offering information pamphlets to peers about birth control because her school doesn't prioritize publicizing available sexual health resources. When a faculty member sees Jules doing this, claiming she is to try to "help," she advises: "For once, try not to make a scene" (Kiely, 2018, p. 20). When Jules pushes back, the teacher instructs: "The last thing you want to do is make this year difficult for yourself. The politicking is done for the day," which "shut [Jules] up" (p. 20). This moment demonstrates how Jules is understood as dangerous, and therefore in this moment, she might be experiencing what Parnitzke Smith and Freyd (2014) call the punishment of whistleblowers.

Finally, some students turn inward to self soothe, find solace, and build community when their schools fail to meet their needs. Several students carve and seek out alternative spaces both on and off campus for relief and respite. As mentioned, in *Honor Code*, a blog is used for sorting out emotional responses to being in boarding school. In *The Mockingbirds*, girls congregate in the exclusive students' Captain's room to ask Alex about what happened the night of her rape and to sort out how to best support her, such as encouraging her to access The Mockingbirds. They pick this place because the staff rarely frequents it. In *Tradition*, because "Fullbrook was so damn claustrophobic, nowhere to go, ever, without feeling that someone was watching you" (p. 228), one of Jules' special places is her tree, her "favorite spot" (p. 35). Her connection to this place is significant:

> The tree was still there. My tree. The tree out on the edge of the bluff, still clinging, not letting go. One day it would fall, or the ground would crumble beneath it, but as long as I'd been at Fullbrook, it had been just as it was now- tenacious, determined, leaning like a body in the breeze, bare branches extended toward the sky [...] I curled into it like it was a lap. I'd never needed to get high here. [...] I was alone, and the moonlight was enough to hold me (p. 159).

The tree is even a site for her sexual expression and pleasure as this is a place where she brings boyfriends for romantic encounters. Even after her former boyfriend attacks her under it, it remains precious to her. In addition to her tree, Fullbrook's boathouse is also a place she and friend Javi escape to when school becomes overwhelming, feeling like themselves there. Jules notices Javi's joy when they escape there, noting how his "happiness was there, oozing all over the place in the boathouse, seeping through the cracks and out into the sand" making them both feel like they can stand "up against everything Fullbrook had to throw at [them], and getting by it all" (p. 112). Finding rest and relief in the nooks and crannies of these schools becomes an important strategy for several students as they cope with all that these places demand of them.

Conclusion

Prior to the Kavanaugh hearings in the fall of 2018, the Head of School at Holton-Arms, Susanna A. Jones, issued a statement regarding Dr. Blasey Ford's allegation. Part of her message included the following: "As a school that empowers women to use their voices, we are proud of this alumna for using hers" (Strauss, 2018, para. 6). While this message was directed towards Dr. Ford's bravery with speaking out about her violent experience at Holton, it also speaks to all prospective and current students, as well as alumni and their loved ones by publically (and "proud[ly]") standing with her. This gestures towards how the violence that occurs at some boarding schools is significant because these places are more than schools – they are communities and homes. As such, stories like *Honor Code*, *The Mockingbirds*, and *Tradition* point to how it is important for schools to make considerable and critical efforts to repair young people and their family's perceptions of the school's role in ethically intervening in rape culture as well as preventing and responding to sexual violence that takes place there. Schools must actively strategize how to exercise the aforementioned institutional courage. We feel strongly that this can happen at both a classroom-level (pedagogically) as well as whole school (policy) level across K-12 and postsecondary contexts.

Individual educators who are invested in combatting sexual violence and resisting rape culture(s) with and alongside students might consider teaching YA sexual assault narratives like the three analyzed here; indeed, such pedagogies have been ongoing for some time with similar YA texts such as Francesca Lia Block's (2000) *The Rose and Beast* and Laurie Halse Anderson's (1999) *Speak* (to name a few), providing necessary curriculum design exemplars and insights. For further insights on teaching YA sexual assault narratives in K-12, see Alsup (2003), Boehm et al. (2021), Colantonio-Yurko et al. (2018), Malo-Juvera (2014), Miller et al. (2023), and Moore & Marshall (2021). For examples situated in postsecondary contexts, see Adams (2020; 2021), Marshall (2009), and Moore (2023; 2022a; 2022b).

These three stories also function as examples of the ways in which literature plays an important role in constructing, deconstructing, and reconstructing the meaning(s) of place – in this case, boarding schools. These literary representations of elite education institutions offer fairly scathing critiques but expose the possible consequences of living in such places, highlighting the necessity for troubling these sites, both fictional and real. These stories do important cultural work in exposing the ways in which boarding schools can foster rape cultures and demonstrate how there are likely many youths using their voices for resistance – that is, we are in agreement with Soep to not romanticize the notion of 'resistance' and understand it as a somewhat slippery thing, "always partial, never complete" (p. 129), "unfold[ing] and transform[ing] over time," with the ever "hovering possibility of disappointment" (p. 130).

Nevertheless, these voices need to be honored and responded to, and further, perhaps much like the Jones quote, recognized proudly by their schools. Institutional betrayal as an analytic frame allows for the interrogations of many kinds of systemic violence(s), particularly the ways in which cultures of sexual violence operate in institutions. Because a major facet of children's and young adult literature is either a kind of school story, includes experiences of school life, or features school-aged youth, institutional betrayal is a generative notion to think with in analyzing such texts.

References

Adams, B. (2021). Consent is not as simple as tea: Student activism against rape culture. *Girlhood Studies, 14*(1), 1-18.

Adams, B. (2020). "I didn't feel confident talking about this issue… But I knew I could talk about a book": Using young adult literature to make sense of #MeToo. *Journal of Literacy Research, 52*(2), 209-230.

Aitchison, D. (2022). x*The school story: Young adult narratives in the age of neoliberalism*. The University of Mississippi.

Alsup, J. (2003). Politizing young adult literature: Reading Anderson's *Speak* as a critical text. *Journal of Adolescent and Adult Literacy, 47*(2), 158-166.

Ayling, P. (2019). *Distinction, exclusivity, and whiteness: Elite Nigerian parents and the international education market*. Springer.

Behaghel, L., de Chaisemartin, C., & Gurgand, M. (2017). Ready for boarding? The effects of a boarding school for disadvantaged students. *American Economic Journal: Applied Economics, 9*(1), 140-164.

Block, F. L. (2000). *The rose and beast*. Harperteen.

Boehm, S., Colantonio-Yurko, K., Olmstead, K., & Miller, H. C. (2021). When princesses become dragons: Critical literacy, damsel, and confronting rape culture in English classrooms. *Girlhood Studies, 14*(3), 72-89.

Brown, E. (2016, March 29). The overwhelming whiteness of U.S. private schools, in six maps and charts. *The Washington Post*. https://www.washingtonpost.com

/news/education/wp/2016/03/29/the-overwhelming-whiteness-of-u-s-private-schools-in-six-maps-and-charts/

Burkhart, K. (2018). *Honor code*. Carolrhoda Lab.

Center for Institutional Courage. (n.d.). Retrieved April 5, 2024, from https://www.institutionalcourage.org/

Colantonio-Yurko, K., Miller, H. C., & Cheveallier, J. (2018). "But she didn't scream": Teaching about sexual assault in young adult literature. *Journal of Language and Literacy Education, 14*(1), 1-16.

Clark, B. L. (1996). *Regendering the school story*. Routledge.

Crawford, L. (2020). *Notes on a silencing*. Little, Brown and Company.

DeTurk, S. (2011). Allies in action: The communicative experiences of people who challenge social injustice on behalf of others. *Communication Quarterly, 59*(5), 569-590.

Duffet, N., & Basset, T. (n.d.). *Trauma, abandonment, and privilege: A guide to the therapeutic work of boarding school survivors*. Routledge.

Epic Reads. (2022, July 19). 19 boarding school books that will make you wish you went to one. Retrieved from https://www.epicreads.com/blog/ya-boarding-school-books/

Fielding, S. (1749/2005). *The governess; or, The little female academy*. Broadview Press.Feir, D. L. (2016). The long-term effects of forcible assimilation policy: The case of Indian boarding schools. *The Canadian Journal of Economics, 49*(2), 433-480.

Fowler, M. J. (2019). Rewriting the school story through racebending in the Harry Potter and Raven Cycle fandoms. *Transformative Works and Cultures, 29*. https://doi.org/10.3983/twc.2019.1492

Freyd, J. J. (1997). Violations of power, adaptive blindness, and betrayal trauma theory. *Feminism and Psychology, 7*, 22-32.

Freyd, J. J. (2021, February 5). Sincere institutional apologies for institutional betrayal are an important step in the institutional-courage direction [Tweet]. Twitter. https://twitter.com/jjfreydcourage/status/1357677144835428352

Freyd, J. J. (n.d.). When sexual assault victims speak out, their institutions often betray them. *The Conversation*. Retrieved July 26, 2022, from https://theconversation.com/when-sexual-assault-victims-speak-out-their-institutions-often-betray-them-87050

Gardner, S., & Crouch, J. (2013). *Maggot Moon*. Candlewick Press.

Gaztambide-Fernández, R. (2009). What is an elite boarding school? *Review of Educational Research, 79*(3), 1090-1128.

Gómez, J. M. (2022). Gender, campus sexual violence, cultural betrayal, institutional betrayal, institutional support in U.S. minority college students: A descriptive study. *Violence Against Women, 28*(1), 93-106.

Gómez, J. M., & Freyd, J. J. (2018). Psychological outcomes of within-group sexual violence: Evidence of cultural betrayal. *Journal of Immigrant & Minority Health, 20*, 1458-1467.

Green, J. (2005). *Looking for Alaska*. Speak.

Gutman, C. (2022, July 19). 50 must-read books set in boarding school. *Book Riot*. https://bookriot.com/books-set-in-boarding-schools/

Hall, R. (2004). It can happen to you: Rape prevention in the age of risk management. *Hypatia, 19*(3), 1-19.

Hubler, A. (2017). It is not enough to speak: Toward a coalitional consciousness in the young adult rape novel. *Children's Literature, 45*, 114-137.

Jack, C. (n.d.). *Recovering boarding school trauma narratives: Christopher Robin Milne as psychological companion on the journey to healing*. Routledge.

Lind, M. N., Adams-Clark, A. A., & Freyd, J. J. (2020). Isn't high school bad enough already? Rates of gender harassment and institutional betrayal in high school and their association with trauma-related symptoms. *PLOS ONE, 15*(8), 1-13.

Malo-Juvera, V. (2014). Speak: The effects of literacy instruction on adolescents' rape myth acceptance. *Research in the Teaching of English, 48*(4), 407-427.

Manne, K. (2020). *Entitled: How male privilege hurts women*. Crown.

Marshall, E. (2009). Girlhood, sexual violence, and agency in Francesca Lia Block's "Wolf". *Children's Literature in Education, 40*, 217-234.

Marshall, E. (2016). Counter storytelling through graphic life writing. *Language Arts, 94*(2), 79-93.

Marshall, E. (2018). *Graphic girlhoods: Visualizing education and violence*. Routledge.

Marshall, E. (2020). Representations of youth, schooling, and education in dystopian YA novels. In M. Cadden, K. Coats, & R. S. Trites (Eds.), *Options for teaching YA fiction* (pp. 191-199). Modern Language Association.

Martin, A. J., Papworth, B., Ginns, P., & Liem, G. A. D. (2014). Boarding school, academic motivation, and psychological well-being: A large-scale investigation. *American Educational Research Journal, 51*(5), 1007-1049.

Miller, H. C., Boehm, S., Colantonio-Yurko, K., Adams, B., & Mertens, G. (2023). Naming and challenging rape culture in English curriculum: A framework for teaching canonical texts with contemporary adaptations. *Changing English*.

Moore, A. (2023a). MeToo moments: Teacher candidates' disclosures of sexual violence. *Action in Teacher Education, 44*(2), 302-314.

Moore, A. (2023b). Creating a canon for change: How teacher candidates demonstrate readiness to reckon with rape culture through reading. *Teaching Education, 34*(2), 131-146.

Moore, A. (2023c). Safe space(s), content (trigger) warnings, and being "careful" with trauma literature pedagogy and rape culture in secondary English teacher education. *Changing English, 29*(1), 77-88.

Moore, A. (2018). Traumatic geographies: Mapping the violent landscapes driving YA rape survivors indoors. *Jeunesse: Young People, Texts, Cultures, 10*(1), 58-84.

Moore, A., & Marshall, E. (2021). Intoxicated masculinity, allyship, and compulsory heterosexuality in YA rape narratives. In K. Moruzi & P. Venzo (Eds.), *Sexuality and sexual identities in literature for young people* (pp. 140-156). Routledge.

Musgrave, P. W. (2015). *From Brown to Bunter: The life and death of the school story*. Routledge.

Mynott, G. (1999). Harry Potter and the public school narrative. *New Review of Children's Literature and Librarianship, 5*(1), 13-27.

Parnitzke Smith, C., & Freyd, J. J. (2013). Dangerous havens: Institutional betrayal exacerbates sexual trauma. *Journal of Traumatic Stress, 26*, 119-124.

Parnitzke Smith, C., & Freyd, J. J. (2014). Institutional betrayal. *American Psychologist, 69*(6), 575-587.

Prout, C., & Abelson, J. (2018). *I have a right to: A high school survivor's story of sexual assault, justice, and hope*. Margaret K. McElderry Books.

Raiker, S. P. (2024, February 9). Boarding school. *Encyclopedia Britannica*. https://www.britannica.com/topic/boarding-school

Ringrose, J., Regehr, K., & Whitehead, S. (2022). "Wanna trade?": Cisheteronormative homosocial masculinity and the normalization of abuse in youth digital sexual image exchange. *Journal of Gender Studies, 31*(2), 243-261.

Rowling, J. K. (1997-2007). *Harry Potter*. Bloomsbury Publishing.

Ryland, J. (2022, July 19). Best YA books set in boarding school. Retrieved from https://www.jenryland.com/ya-books-boarding-school-shenanigans/

Simpson, N. (2018). *Finding our way home: Women's accounts of being sent to boarding schools*. Routledge.

Schaverien, J. (2015). *Boarding school syndrome: The psychological trauma of the "privileged" child*. Routledge.

Soep, E. (2011). Resistance. In N. Lesko & S. Talburt (Eds.), *Keywords in youth studies: Tracing affects, movements, knowledges* (pp. 127-130). Routledge.

Strauss, V. (2018, September 17). High school attended by Kavanaugh's accuser says it is "proud" of her for speaking up. *The Washington Post*. Retrieved from https://www.washingtonpost.com/education/2018/09/17/high-school-attended-by-kavanaughs-accuser-comes-out-support-her/

Stein, N. (2005). Still no laughing matter: Sexual harassment in K-12 schools. In E. Buchwald, P. Fletcher, & M. Roth (Eds.), *Transforming a rape culture* (pp. 58-71). Milkweed Editions.

Walden, T. (2018). *On a sunbeam*. First Second.

Whitney, D. (2010). *The Mockingbirds*. Little Brown and Company.

Social, Communal, and Familial: Examining Isolation through Setting Analysis in Sexual Assault Young Adult Literature

Shelby Boehm, Illinois State University, Henry Cody Miller, SUNY Brockport, and Lorelei Starkey, Illinois State University

Introduction

In this chapter we demonstrate how teachers can approach teaching setting in a way that surfaces gendered power dynamics and the aftermath of sexual assault using young adult literature (YAL). More than merely the location of the story, a critical analysis of setting can reveal sociological, cultural, and political features of a narrative and how those features impact individual characters (Beach et al., 2021; Miller, 2018). Understanding the gendered undercurrents of YAL can inform which texts teachers select for curricular purposes (Cleveland & Durand, 2014) and what pedagogical moves teachers make when positioning and teaching books (Alsup, 2003). Specifically, we analyze setting through the concept of isolation as it pertains to sexual assault and sexual violence. Katz (2019) identified three folding layers of isolation that stems from sexual violence: first, the perpetrator physically isolates the survivor in order to enact the violence; then, friends, family, and institutions can question the validity of the survivor's story and the survivor can turn to silence as a tactic; finally, the survivor may feel constant anxious feelings of unsafety and want to avoid public spaces, which furthers the social isolation. The second layer, which focuses on social, communal, and familiar features, is especially pertinent to our suggestions.

We highlight three books that narrate how sexual assault survivors are relegated to isolation in the aftermath of sexual violence: *Dear Medusa* by Olivia A. Cole (2023), *Some Boys* by Patty Blount (2014), and *The Way I Used to Be* by Amber Smith (2017). Taken together, these books work as a panoply of texts that address sexual violence and rape culture in order to "engender promising new ways to reframe the literature classroom as a site for dynamic solidarity and resistance(s) against rape culture" (Moore, 2022, p. 79). Our focus on setting as a sociological site that creates insiders and outsiders in the aftermath of sexual violence works to highlight the systemic dimensions of rape culture and sexual violence rather than solely attending to the survivor and perpetuator (Altrows, 2019). In this chapter, we detail the three books and provide activities and questions that can move the setting of a book from a matter of literary comprehension into a site of interrogatory analysis.

Positionality

We approach this research question as three able-bodied cisgender white teachers and teacher educators. Shelby and Cody have incorporated YAL that features sexual assault as a major plot point across the spectrum of courses we have taught ranging from high school English to graduate teacher education. Lorelei has led a student organization aimed at raising the visibility of rape culture on her college campus, and as a secondary English preservice teacher, she is also interested in taking up such work in her future classroom. As educators inside and outside of classrooms, we advocate for the inclusion of affirmative consent in sex education, revisions in dress codes to address victim blaming mentality, inclusion of LGBTQ topics in human development and sex education units, and other measures we believe could challenge the logics of sexual assault in our educational institutions.

This project stems from our own teaching practices as well as how we position ourselves as advocates on our respective campuses. Additionally, we recognize that our work must also be reflective and contested. Thus, we must habitually interrogate how systems of oppression such as racism, ableism, classism, homo- and transphobia and other forms of harm shape how we approach our work in teaching and researching about sexual assault and young adult literature. We are committed to a stance of continual learning, and work to incorporate recent research and writings to broaden, deepen, and reorient our views on young adult literature and sexual assault.

Young Adult Literature, Sexual Assault, and Pedagogical Potential

Numerous scholars have called for YAL to be a pedagogical avenue to discuss, examine, and work towards ending sexual assault, harassment, and violence (Alsup, 2003; Cart, 1996; Cleveland & Durand, 2014; Colantonio-Yurko, et al., 2018; Jackett, 2007; Malo-Juvera, 2014a, 2014b; Miller et al., 2022; Park, 2012; Pattee, 2004). With a focus on language, meaning, and texts, Johnson and Kerkhoff (2018) argue that literary studies are ripe for addressing the #MeToo movement and the "nuance between unethical and illegal behavior" (p. 14). Subsequently, other YAL scholars have seen the genre as a potential site for addressing key ideas and terminology surrounding sexual assault with secondary and post-secondary students, who are often socialized into harmful beliefs about survivors. For instance, both Park's (2012) study of middle schoolers reading *Speak* (Anderson, 1999) and Malo-Juvera (2014b)'s study of students reading the same title found students shifting their thinking and disrupting rape myths regarding individuals' actions and behaviors when guided with intentional pedagogies. While considering individuals is important, students also need to understand how systemic forces uphold and give credence to these dangerous misconceptions regarding sexual violence and victim blaming (Adams, 2020), especially since YAL featuring rape frequently reifies neoliberal beliefs about the individuals rather than addressing feminist concerns about the systemic issues (Altrows, 2019).

The potential of YAL in developing students' understanding of assault and rape spans curricular forms and subgenres of young adult literature. For example, some literacy scholars have called for pairing YAL with canonical texts to address how sexual assault and violence manifest across chronological contexts (Colantonio-Yurko, et al., 2018; Malo-Juvera, 2014a). Other scholarship has considered how fictional athletes perpetuate sexual assault (Boehm et al., 2020), how genres like fantasy address sexual assault (Boehm et al., 2021; Herb, 2021; Spiering & Amato, 2022), and how YA film adaptations impact families' and caregivers' understanding of contemporary conversations about assault (Walter & Boyd, 2019).

This chapter takes up two concepts for teachers to consider when teaching books that include sexual assault: setting analysis and isolation. We draw on prior work to inform our chapter. Previous scholarship has asked educators to move beyond setting analysis as mere geography when teaching narratives that feature sexual assault. For instance, teachers can critically examine setting by considering how gendered norms, power dynamics, and histories shape how sexual assault is discussed, understood, and addressed within a narrative's setting (Boehm, et al., 2021; Colantonio-Yurko, et al., 2018). Scholarship that has examined how sympathy is constructed through social gendered norms informs how we consider isolation as a social act of continuing violence after a character is assaulted (Miller, et al., 2022). Our suggestions within these two concepts draw on literary (setting analysis) and sociological (isolation) ideas to inform teaching YAL that includes sexual assault.

Like any emerging body of scholarship, this collection has its limitations: the majority of scholarship relating to sexual assault in YAL has centered victims who are mostly white, cisgender, and heterosexual females. In writing about a lack of representation in young adult rape novels, Hubler (2017) argues that "narrators who are Black, poor, gay, or intellectually disabled articulate the experiences and insights of disadvantaged social groups" that shed light on the "ways in which gender interacts with other social institutions to structure violence" (p. 115). Recent scholarship points to the need for publishers to tell other stories. For instance, Menefee (2024) has examined how YAL addresses sexual and reproductive choice of Black teenage girls, including how titles narrate sexual violence and its aftermath. We agree that this genre needs to center the experiences of victims outside of white middle-class cisgender heterosexual characters. We want to note our own limitation to this chapter: the three books we analyze in the remainder of this chapter reflect the broader trend of YAL texts that provide "moral attention to women with dominant gender, racial, and sexual identities" (Miller, et al., 2022, p. 316). Additionally, one of the books we discuss below, *Some Boys* (Blount, 2014), features a white girl protagonist who unintentionally reinforces an Islamophobic belief about Muslim women in her attempt to make a protest statement, which speaks to the ways white feminism often perpetuates harm against women of color (Ezaydi, 2023). We must continue to interrogate the ways oppression replicates even among a sub-genre that seeks to challenge rape culture and critique sexist structures.

The Books

The three young adult texts we highlight in this chapter offer stories of survivors of sexual violence who have become outcasts within their contexts. Although the perpetrators have varying positionalities (e.g., teacher, peers) within the plot of the novels, each book offers avenues for understanding power dynamics around assault that lead to the survivor's isolation in particular settings.

Dear Medusa by Olivia A. Cole (2023)

Alicia is assaulted by a popular teacher at her school. Because Alicia was sexually active prior to the assault, her best friend, Sarah, struggles to understand Alicia as a victim. Sarah uses her religious views to frame Alicia's assault as a consequence of impurity, and their friendship ends. As Alicia navigates social isolation as a result of her trauma, she receives anonymous notes in her locker from another student assaulted by the popular teacher. The majority of the book takes place at Marshall High School, where Alicia is a rising junior.

Some Boys by Patty Blount (2014)

While attending a party, Grace is drinking and later assaulted by a popular peer, Zach. She is found bleeding and unconscious. After Zach is accused of raping Grace, he shares a video of them together to purport consensual sex. Her peers then call Grace derogatory words, and she struggles to be believed. Zach's status as the school's golden boy furthers Grace's isolation from her school community. The majority of the book takes place at Grace's high school.

The Way I Used to Be **by Amber Smith (2017)**
Eden is assaulted by her older brother's best friend, Kevin. Afterwards, Eden is shamed into silence as Kevin taunts that no one would believe her. The story then follows the impact of the assault on Eden's four years of high school. Back at college, Kevin is accused of raping another victim. Eden's brother and family dismiss the accusations, contending that Kevin would never assault someone. This reaction advanced Eden's isolation from her family and peers. The majority of the book takes place at Eden's high school over the course of her secondary schooling experience.

Teaching Setting Using Sexual Assault Young Adult Literature

It is important for teachers to recognize that these novels might be triggering and thus we encourage educators to provide students with trigger warnings. Discussions around sexual assault and violence can cause discomfort, confusion, or even guilt; reactions will differ drastically, even among survivors. Striving to create safe spaces to discuss sexual assault in classrooms is nuanced and complicated, but small, implementable steps can make a difference, including considering classroom contexts, students' experiences, and institutional resources prior to engaging in the type of teaching (Moore, 2022). Teachers should work to ensure that students are provided with statistics and definitions of sexual violence prior to engaging with texts, this ensures that they have a "strong foundation" of concepts (Jackett, 2007; Malo-Juvera, 2014b).

Once foundational concepts and community norms for entering conversations around sexual assault have been established, YAL can be used as a vehicle for naming the systems (and the resulting spaces/settings) that perpetuate rape culture as a pedagogical move to center survivors in conversations on sexual violence (Melik, 2023). In this section, we offer teaching suggestions for facilitating discussions on setting and isolation using YAL featuring sexual violence. Using various kinds of isolation—social, communal, and familial—as a throughline for

Table 5.1 Types of Isolation

	Social Isolation	Communal Isolation	Familial Isolation
Definition	Lack of connection with peers, especially close and trusted friends.	Disconnect between self and sense of community or belonging in a defined space, such as neighborhood or school.	Disengagement and distance from family members, such as siblings or parents.
Settings	Work, Home, School	Neighborhood, School, Sports	Home, School

Table 5.2 Examples of Social Isolation

Dear Medusa (Cole, 2023)	Some Boys (Blount, 2014)	The Way I Used to Be (Smith, 2017)
Alicia's best friend, Sarah, shames her for sexual behavior and doubts her innocence after the assault. Sarah ends their friendship.	Grace's best friend, Miranda, ends their friendship after Grace is assaulted by Zac. Miranda has a crush on Zac and considers Grace at fault for her assault.	Eden is isolated from her peers because of her sexual activity.
When I started sleeping with guys, my friendship with Sarah became an hourglass. (p. 16)		Two girls write things about Eden in all of the school bathrooms: "You know–slut, whore, skank, bitch, whatever. All true, so just take your pick…" (p. 88).
…all I can think about is what Sarah would say: There you go, lamb to slaughter, you knew why he called you to his class, you knew when he started to close the door but you still sat there quiet so that must mean you wanted to be there, that some part of you likes it, likes him. You already sleep with everyone else, why is this any different? (p. 89-90)	"Oh my God, we just want you to know we don't believe her. You're such a great guy, Zac." Miranda puts a hand on Zac's arm. (p. 30)	

reading supports analysis of how setting can influence a character's emotions, reactions, and decision-making, among other plot considerations. In Table 5.1, we provide definitions for isolation types and the settings in which they occur.

In tables 5.2, 5.3, and 5.4 we offer examples of these isolation types across settings from three YAL novels: *Dear Medusa* (Cole, 2023), *Some Boys* (Blount, 2014), and *The Way I Used to Be* (Smith, 2017). To support classroom integration of these texts, we also provide possible questions to guide discussion about each type of isolation.

Possible classroom discussion questions to explore social isolation include: In what ways does the survivor experience isolation from peers or other similar groups? How does social isolation influence before, during, or the aftermath of the assault? How does the setting contribute to the survivor's isolation? In what ways does social isolation perpetuate rape culture? How does social isolation impact the survivor's overall characterization in the text?

Possible classroom discussion questions to explore communal isolation include: How does the survivor experience disconnect from their community? In what ways are they positioned as an insider or outsider in their community? How does communal isolation impact before, during, or the aftermath of the

Table 5.3 Examples of Communal Isolation

Dear Medusa (Cole, 2023)	Some Boys (Blount, 2014)	The Way I Used to Be (Smith, 2017)
The teacher who assaulted Alicia (referred to as the Colonel because of a Halloween costume he wears) is well-loved in the school community.	Zac, who is popular and perceived as the school's golden boy, knows his status in the community protects him from the rape accusations. He continues to harass Grace.	Rape culture at Eden's school is common and unrelenting. Two jocks harass Eden in the hallway, asking if she wants to be in their sex film, telling her "…we hear you have a lot of experience in that, uh… genre… you have excellent references" (p. 171).
Ms. Gladstone talks to me like she loves me, but when she asks Is something going on I still can't tell her because behind her on the shelf is a picture of her and the Colonel, hands linked… (p. 24)	My dad keeps telling me to stand up to all of Zac's defenders, but it's the entire bus—the entire *school*—versus me. (p. 15)	
My biology teacher hurt me and if I was smarter I could find a clever metaphor about chemistry that tells why and how but the simplest way to say it is that I was a student but he saw a rabbit and no one will believe me because he's the most beloved wolf in school. (p. 74)		

assault? In what ways does the setting contribute to the survivor's ostracization? In what ways does communal isolation facilitate rape culture? How does communal isolation impact the survivor's overall characterization in the text?

Possible classroom discussion questions to explore familial isolation include: In what ways does the survivor experience isolation from their family? How does familial isolation affect before, during, or the aftermath of the assault? In what ways does the setting contribute to the survivor's alienation? In what ways does familiar isolation support rape culture? How does familial isolation influence the survivor's overall characterization in the text?

In addition to the definitions and guiding questions above, below we describe three practices for critically analyzing setting with students to consider how isolation operates within these texts. We understand that context will shape the decisions an educator makes. For instance, how a ninth-grade English teacher approaches these conversations could be different from an undergraduate

Table 5.4 Examples of Familial Isolation

Dear Medusa (Cole, 2023)	Some Boys (Blount, 2014)	The Way I Used to Be (Smith, 2017)
Alicia's brother, David, is part of different social groups that take priority over their sibling relationship. It feels like a black hole has opened in my throat as I realize the things people say about me have reached my brother's ears, and he would rather spit it all back at me than choose not to hear. (p. 193)	Grace's parents victim-blame her for her assault, specifically pointing to what she wears. "Well, honey, you wear a lot of leather and spikes and tight clothes, and that just tells boys—…Damn it, Grace, you made it easy! You were out at night in the woods, drunk, and dressed like…like—" (p. 267)	Eden's brother, Caelin's, best friend Kevin is accused of raping a girl at his college. Eden's parents and brother do not believe the victim. Caelin tells us, "It's his girlfriend. It just— it doesn't even make sense— I mean, why would he need to rape someone he was already sleeping with?" (p. 313)

instructor. We offer suggestions for when each practice could be enacted through a curricular unit or module. However, we stress our suggestions should be malleable to the particular contexts of a classroom. Yet, we believe there are some guidelines that are applicable across contexts. First, secondary and post-secondary educators should include content warnings before assigning and reading books that feature sexual assault as well as providing resources for students who may need additional support (e.g., guidance counselors for high schoolers, counseling centers for college students) (Colantonio-Yurko, et al., 2018; Moore, 2022). Additionally, educators should outline the reasoning for teaching titles with sexual assault when introducing the readings to students. We urge that educators engage in constant reflection as they introduce a title, teach a title, and conclude a unit. Considering what worked, what tensions existed, and how students responded can support teachers in developing trauma-informed, care-oriented practices.

Demystifying Sexual Assault and Violence

While reading sexual assault young adult literature, we see possibilities for demystifying sexual assault and violence further by sharing key information, such as definitions of common terms, statistics, and other relevant knowledge depending on the context. For instance, students could research and design public service announcements (Early, 2022) that provide such information ideally to an authentic context, such as a school or local community site at the end of a curricular unit or module. This teaching solution would support a survivor-centered approach to framing sexual violence with practice using inclusive language that prevents causing harm (Melik, 2023). When using survivor-centered framing through inclusive language, victim blaming myths are more likely to be eliminated, which creates a supportive environment for others to reflect on their experiences without the fear of being blamed or judged as a survivor of sexual violence. This type of activity could connect a literary analysis of sexual assault with action-oriented steps students can take in their community or on campus (Boehm, et al., 2021). Providing students with an opportunity for action at the end of a curricular unit or module can position students as critical readers and critical agents.

Locating Victim Blaming as a Contextual Feature

Because sexual assault young adult literature often features characters with a victim blaming mentality, we offer a teaching solution for tracing these myths as a contextual feature within the setting of a novel. Students could map moments of victim blaming by identifying characters who place blame on survivors of assault and the ensuing reactions from survivors throughout the reading process. This activity would illustrate how such attitudes permeate the setting of the text, offering insight beyond the individual dimensions of rape culture. While the reactions people have to issues of sexual violence are often connected to the ways in which they have individually experienced or viewed sexual violence in the past, reactions to sexual violence must attend to the systemic conditions to illustrate the many dimensions of rape culture (Altrows, 2019). Educators can note that victim blaming is a concept that will be traced throughout the reading process and shape classroom discussions. By addressing victim blaming as a contextual feature throughout the reading process, students can analyze how victim blaming mentalities stretch across time and space to crystalize ideas about sexual assault within particular settings. As an extension activity, teachers could invite students to locate victim blaming myths in texts of their choosing.

Alleviating Isolation through Community and Witnessing

We also urge the teachers to view sexual assault young adult literature as a site for imagining more just futures for the real worlds students live in. For instance, sexual assault narratives have been theorized as sites of bystander intervention (Adams et al., 2022) and rewriting scenes from young adult literature can be one way for students to imagine action steps they can take in their real lives (Boehm et al., 2021). In that vein, our final teaching solution involves imagining what characters could do to reduce isolation and build community with the characters who survived sexual assault. Educators can select key scenes from the novels to imagine alternative approaches secondary characters could do to support survivor characters. For instance, scenes in which characters discuss their assaults with other characters or scenes in which a character victim blames could be generative parts to consider different paths for characters to take. Educators can prompt students to imagine what characters could do to reduce isolation after each key scene. Alternatively, educators could pull key scenes and have students imagine new actions after completing the book. When actualized, such envisioning could lead to affirming spaces for survivors, where survivors could build connections with others with similar experiences and have a network with whom they can talk to openly and freely about the effects of rape culture on their lives.

Further Considerations

Survivor-centered approaches to teaching about sexual violence and rape culture are important for modeling the types of responses we hope young people take up in their own work to resist rape culture. As stories of survivors and perpetrators of sexual assault continue to surface in the mainstream, we wonder about other pathways for analyzing common literary conventions that illuminate facets of rape culture as a systemic dimension rather than an individual problem. An analysis of characterization with sexual assault young adult literature, for example, could support the identification of direct or indirect features, such as sexism or misogyny, that preserve rape culture in the novel. Additionally, analyzing tropes that appear in sexual assault young adult literature like "saving the princess" could offer pathways for how popular narratives become harmful beliefs. Such directions, which begin with typical approaches to literary analysis in English language arts, present methods for moving beyond to critically analyze literary conventions as a form of solidarity with survivors and resistance to rape culture.

References

Adams, B. (2020). "I didn't feel confident talking about this issue… but I knew I could talk about a book": Using young adult literature to make sense of #MeToo. *Journal of Literacy Research, 52*(2), 209-230.

Adams, B., Colantonio-Yurko, K., Miller, C., & Boehm, S. (2022). Beyond perpetrators, victims, and survivors: Young adult literature as bystander intervention education. *ALAN Review, 49*(3), 42-51.

Alsup, J. (2003). Politicizing young adult literature: Reading Anderson's Speak as a critical text. *Journal of Adolescent & Adult Literacy, 47*(2), 158-166.

Altrows, A. (2019). Silence and the regulation of feminist anger in young adult rape fiction. *Girlhood Studies, 12*(2), 1-16.

Anderson, L. H. (1999). *Speak*. Penguin Group.

Beach, R., Appleman, D., Fecho, B., & Simon, R. (2021). *Teaching literature to adolescents (4th ed)*. Routledge.

Blount, P. (2014). *Some boys*. Sourcebooks Fire.

Boehm, S., Colantonio-Yurko, K.C., Olmstead, K. & Miller, H.C. (2020). Athlete as agitator, assaulter, and armor: Sports, identity, and sexual assault in young adult literature. *Study and Scrutiny: Research on Young Adult Literature, 4*(2), 31-56.

Boehm, S., Colantonio-Yurko, K. C., Olmstead, K., & Miller, H.C. (2021). When princesses become dragons: Critical literacy, Damsel, and confronting rape culture in English classrooms. *Girlhood Studies, 14*(3), 72-89.

Cart, M. (1996). *From romance to realism: 50 years of growth and change in young adult literature*. Harper Collins.

Cleveland, E., & Durand, E. S. (2014). Critical representations of sexual assault in young adult literature. *The Looking Glass: New Perspectives on Children's Literature, 17*(3).

Colantonio-Yurko, K., Miller, H. C., & Cheveallier, J. (2018). "But she didn't scream": Teaching about sexual assault in young adult literature. *Journal of Language and Literacy Education, 14*(1), 1-16.

Cole, O. A. (2023). *Dear medusa*. Labyrinth Road.

Early, J. S. (2022). *Next generation genres: Teaching writing for civic and academic engagement* (First edition). Norton Professional Books.

Ezaydi, S. (2023, Mar 13). What is white feminism and how does it harm women of colour?. *Mashable*. Retrieved from https://mashable.com/article/white-feminism-explained.

Herb, A. (2021). (Para)normalizing rape culture possession as rape in young adult paranormal romance. *Girlhood Studies, 14*(1), 68-84.

Hubler, A. E. (2017). It is not enough to speak: Toward a coalitional consciousness in the young adult rape novel. *Children's Literature, 45*(1), 114-137.

Jackett, M. (2007). Something to speak about: Addressing sensitive issues through literature. *English Journal, 96*(4), 102-105.

Johnson, T. S., & Kerkhoff, S. (2018). # MeToo in English education. *English Education, 51*(1), 4-16.

Katz, L. (2019, Aug 18). *Why victims of sexual trauma feel alone and isolated*. Psychology today. https://www.psychologytoday.com/us/blog/healing-sexual-trauma/201908/why-victims-sexual-trauma-feel-alone-and-isolated

Malo-Juvera, V. (2014a). Speaking to the classics. *SIGNAL, 37*(2), 7-11.

Malo-Juvera, V. (2014b). Speak. The effect of literacy instruction on adolescents' rape myth acceptance. *Research in the Teaching of English, 48*(4), 407-27.

Melik, A. (2023, Apr 3). *Centering survivors: A resource for families and educators in responding to sexual violence*. Learning for Justice. https://www.learningforjustice.org/magazine/center-survivors-a-resource-for-families-and-educators-in-responding-to-sexual-violence

Menefee, D. L. (2024). "Well, that's what she gets...": Black teenage girls' sexual and reproductive choice in young adult literature. *Research on Diversity in Youth Literature, 5*(2), Article 3.

Miller, C. (2018). Teaching the intersections of religion, nationality, and sexuality: LGBTQ Muslim voices in Sara Farizan's novels. *SIGNAL, 42*(2), 8-17.

Miller, C., Boehm, S., Yurko, K.C., & Adams, B. (2022). Himpathy, herasure, and down girl moves: A critical content analysis of sexual assault in young adult literature. *Journal of Literacy Research, 54*(3), 298-321.

Moore, A. (2022). Safe space(s), content (trigger) warnings, and being "care-ful" with trauma literature pedagogy and rape culture in secondary English teacher education. *Changing English: Studies in Culture and Education, 25*(1), 1-11.

Park, J. Y. (2012). Re-imaging reader-response in middle and secondary schools: Early adolescent girls' critical and communal reader responses to the young adult novel Speak. *Children's Literature in Education, 43*(3), 191- 212.

Pattee, A. (2004). Disturbing the peace: The function of young adult literature and the case of Catherine Atkin's When Jeff Comes Come. *Children's Literature in Education, 35*(3), 241-255.

Smith, A. (2017). *The way I used to be*. Margaret K. Mcelderry Books.

Spiering, J., & Amato, N. A. (2022). "Nothing to do but be borne and steered": Unpacking feminist scripts in Elana Arnold's Damsel. *The International Journal of Young Adult Literature, 3*(1), 1-19. https://doi.org/10.24877/IJYAL.76

Walter, B., & Boyd, A. S. (2019). A threat or just a book? Analyzing responses to Thirteen Reasons Why in a discourse community. *Journal of Adolescent & Adult Literacy, 62*(6), 615-623.

Male Youth-Athletes as Victims of Sexual Violence in Recommended Sports-Related Young Adult Literature

Mark A. Lewis, James Madison University and
Luke Rodesiler, Purdue University Fort Wayne

Sexual violence is exceedingly common in the United States (U.S.). Statistics from the Rape, Abuse & Incest National Network (RAINN, 2023b) show that there are almost 500,000 reported incidents of sexual violence every year in the U.S. The majority of the victims— approximately 59%— are aged 12 to 34. Within this age bracket, 8 out of 10 juvenile victims are girls, which means about 20% of juvenile victims are male. Sexual violence is so pervasive that it creeps into various facets of everyday life, from school to sport. Regarding the latter, the sports world is a site where rape culture has been incessant in the U.S. and beyond. That much is evident, for the United Nations Educational, Scientific and Cultural Organization (UNESCO, 2023) reported that approximately 21% of professional female athletes and 11% of their male counterparts have experienced some form of sexual abuse as a child in sport (p. 6). UNESCO's statistics, like RAINN's, do not account for individuals who opt not to disclose the sexual violence committed against them, so we presume these numbers are rather modest figures. Regardless, these statistics underscore the prevalence of sexual violence in youth sports.

When the topic of rape culture arises, one's mind may turn to heinous acts committed against women—and understandably so, given the aforementioned statistics from RAINN and UNESCO respectively. Yet, UNESCO's findings about male athletes and news stories about alleged acts of sexual violence committed against male high school athletes by a substitute teacher (Bruner, 2023), by a coach (Reid, 2023), by an athletic trainer (Schilken, 2024), and by peers (Jurado, 2023) drew our attention. As scholars with a shared interest in stories of sports, we began to wonder how such conflicts are depicted in contemporary realistic fiction written for secondary-aged youth. Subsequently, in this chapter intended for an audience of scholars and practicing teachers alike, we examine how male youth-athletes who endure sexual violence are portrayed in the novels *Leverage* (Cohen, 2011), *Swagger* (Deuker, 2013), and *Boy Toy* (Lyga, 2007). We begin by reviewing related scholarship and outlining our analytical methods, continue with what we found in these young adult literature (YAL) selections, and conclude with a discussion on the significance of our work for both adult and youth readers.

Sexual Violence in Young Adult Literature

Over the last decade, scholars have examined YAL to explore representations of sexual violence against young women. For example, Miller et al. (2022) explored how YAL that include stories about sexual violence might engage in misogynistic practices that ultimately privilege male-oriented perspectives of sexual assault. In particular, they found that many of the characters in the YAL they examined either intentionally or unintentionally allow '*him*pathy,' or sympathizing with male perpetrators rather than female victims and survivors, and '*her*asure,' or silencing women's stories in favor of men's stories, to influence their perspectives on incidents of sexual violence. These perspectives include how the circumstances of the assault are re-told, how friends of both perpetrators and victims react to the assault, and how justice, if any, is served. Other scholars have lauded YAL's utility as a platform for talking about sexual violence with youth (Charles, 2019; Colantonio-Yurko et al., 2018), helping readers understand the #MeToo movement (Adams, 2020; Cleveland & Durand, 2014), and complicating young people's acceptance of rape mythology (Malo-Juvera, 2014). This chapter aims to contribute to this discussion on the utility of YAL as a tool for building understanding about this complex sociopolitical issue.

Even more pertinent to the focus of our chapter, Boehm et al. (2020) identified distinct identities worn by male youth-athletes who are portrayed as perpetrators across several sports-related texts. Some of these characters act as sexual agitators who engage in sexually-related harassment and verbal abuse toward women in their social circles. Other characters are portrayed as assaulters who are physically and sexually violent against female characters. As well, Boehm et al. (2020) found that male youth-athletes in these stories are able to use their athlete status as armor that shields them from any accusations or consequences. Often, these male youth-athlete characters wear all three of these identities.

We seek to build upon scholarship that explored incidents of sexual violence perpetrated against young women in YAL by focusing on depictions of male youth-athletes who suffer sexual abuse or sexual assault in recommended literature for young adults. With this study, we set out to identify sports-related YAL that includes sexual violence toward male youth-athletes and to examine the messages these stories communicate to readers as one way to address the issue of sexual violence. Two research questions inform our study: 1) How are male youth-athletes who suffer sexual violence depicted in recommended sports-related YAL? 2) How is victimhood portrayed in these stories?

Methods

This section describes the methods we used to find texts that could help us investigate our guiding research questions, details the methods we used to analyze the three texts we selected, and establishes our positionalities as researchers.

Text Selection and Analysis

When launching this study, we first sought to identify relevant texts by reviewing award/honor lists and websites that publish professional book reviews. The lists we reviewed included the American Library Association's Book Awards, the International Literacy Association's Children's and Young Adult Book Awards, and the Young Adult Library Services Association's (YALSA) Book Awards and Book Lists. The book-review websites we searched are published by respected outlets, including *Booklist, Kirkus Reviews, Publishers Weekly,* and *School Library Journal*. As we searched for relevant texts, we focused on five criteria to guide selection: (a) contemporary realistic fiction deemed appropriate for secondary-aged youth; (b) multiple scenes depicting the protagonist engaged in athletic competition; (c) a plot that involves the sexual abuse or sexual assault of a male youth-athlete; (d) publication within 20 years of our study's launch (i.e., 2003-2022); and (e) an award, honor-list recognition, or starred review from at least one of the aforementioned outlets or organizations.

We included each criterion for text selection with intentionality. The first three criteria were necessary to address our guiding research questions. That is, we could not examine the depiction of male youth-athletes who suffer sexual violence in sports-related YAL if the texts selected are not considered appropriate for teenagers, do not prominently feature youth engaged in sports, and do not tell stories involving sexual violence perpetrated against male youth-athletes. Regarding the first criterion, which involves age appropriateness, we relied on the publisher's suggestion or, as necessary, the suggestion offered in a professional book review from a reputable outlet. Additionally, the second criterion proved helpful when it came to defining what counts as "sports-related." For instance, Bill Konigsberg's (2019) *The Music of What Happens* features a protagonist who reveals that he is a survivor of sexual assault and talks about playing baseball, yet no scenes in the story involve him actually playing the game. In that way, the book stood apart from others we reviewed that were more obviously sports-related, for they featured multiple scenes of youth-athletes engaged in their chosen sport, so that criterion guided our decision to exclude Konigsberg's novel from this study. The fourth criterion positioned us to consider titles that were published relatively recently, and we included the fifth criterion based on the logic that awards and recognition tend to result in greater publicity, which stands to increase the likelihood that students will encounter the text in question.

Employing the aforementioned criteria, we selected *Leverage* (Cohen, 2011), *Swagger* (Deuker, 2013), and *Boy Toy* (Lyga, 2007) for our study investigating the depiction of male youth-athletes who suffer sexual violence in recommended sports-related YAL and the portrayal of victimhood in these stories. Table 1 presents a brief synopsis of each novel and the recognition each novel has received.

To address our guiding research questions, we conducted a thematic analysis (Prasad, 2002; Schwandt, 2015). We started by reading each story independently and making notes to aid analysis and support the development of themes. While reading and re-reading the novels, we focused our thematic analyses on the depictions of characters before they were sexually abused or sexually assaulted to address the first research question, and we focused our thematic analyses on the depiction of these characters after they were sexually abused or sexually assaulted to build understanding about the portrayals of victimhood, which is central to the second research question. When analyzing these depictions, we concentrated on characterization conveyed through descriptions of their physical traits, their thoughts, their actions, and their dialogue, as well as how these characters are perceived by others. After reading all three novels, we looked across them, recording similarities and differences in relation to each guiding

Table 6.1 Selected Works of Sports-Related YAL Featuring a Male Victim of Sexual Violence

Title	Brief Synopsis	Recognition
Leverage (Cohen, 2011)	Kurt Brodsky, a football player, and Danny Meehan, a gymnast, become unlikely allies after they witness a small band of football players sexually assaulting gymnast Ronnie Gunderson on school grounds.	YALSA, a division of the American Library Association, made Cohen's story a 2012 Top Ten Best Fiction for Young Adults selection. In 2011, the novel was a Booklist Editors' Choice: Books for Youth selection, and it also received a starred review from Booklist.
Swagger (Deuker, 2013)	Jonas Dolan is relying on teammate Levi Rawdon to help him earn a basketball scholarship, but Levi's performance suffers after he is sexually abused by an adult they trusted.	YALSA made Deuker's novel a 2015 Quick Picks for Reluctant Readers selection.
Boy Toy (Lyga, 2007)	Josh Mendel, a college baseball prospect, is preparing for the next stage of his life, but he remains haunted by the sexual abuse perpetrated by his history teacher five years prior.	YALSA made Lyga's novel a 2008 Best Books for Young Adults selection. The book also received starred reviews from *Kirkus Reviews*, *Publishers Weekly*, and *School Library Journal*.

research question. Then, with our independent analyses complete, we compiled our notes, reconvened, and talked through interpretations and discrepancies to establish shared understandings of the thematic messages presented in the stories.

Researchers' Positionalities

We come to this project with histories of working with youth in schools and in sports. We are former middle and high school English language arts teachers and coaches, and these identities inform our interests in sports-related YAL. Moreover, we identify as White, cisgender men, and we are cognizant of the privileges these identities afford us as scholars and as citizens. Aware of our privileges, we strive to promote a more just world by intentionally taking up scholarship that supports the critical study of YAL, of sports culture, and of our global society. That work continues with this project, in which we aim to shine a light on sexual violence perpetrated against male youth-athletes—both on the page and in the world.

Male Youth-Athletes and Victimhood in Selected Sports-Related YAL

In this section, we present our analytic findings for each research question, addressing the first question by focusing on the depiction of male youth-athlete characters before they suffer sexual violence and addressing the second question by focusing on the presentation of these characters after they are assaulted or abused.

Depictions of Male Youth-Athletes

Across the three novels, the male youth-athletes who suffer sexual violence play a variety of sports—basketball, gymnastics, and baseball—for school-sanctioned teams. In *Swagger*, Levi Rawdon is a key player on the high school basketball team. Ronnie Gunderson is a high school gymnast in *Leverage*, and Josh Mendel is a star slugger for his high school's baseball team in *Boy Toy*. Their status as athletes is where the similarities end.

Levi is a gentle, deeply religious, soft-spoken teenager who enjoys the outdoors and struggles in school. According to protagonist Jonas Dolan, who first meets Levi shortly after moving into his neighborhood, Levi's soft voice and demeanor belie his size; standing at approximately 6' 6", he is "six inches taller and thirty pounds heavier [than Jonas]" (Deuker, 2013, p. 49). Based on their early encounters, Jonas describes Levi as "simple, like a child" (p. 64), for Levi perceives tackling in the game of football as sinful, insists on using titles of courtesy (i.e., "Mr." and "Coach") when referring to their head basketball coach, and plays on the floor with his younger sisters. This child-like demeanor only encourages some of Levi's teammates to give him a hard time about his academic performance by calling him "Dumb-Dumb" or "Double D" (p. 60), a pair of pejorative nicknames that he passively accepts. Contrary to some of his teammates, Levi also refuses to participate in a summer party—a party thrown by Ryan Hartwell, the man who becomes his coach, his tutor, and his abuser—because alcohol and pornography are present. Levi's passivity and difference from his teammates are likely reasons that Hartwell identifies him as a target for sexual abuse.

Ronnie is represented as small in stature but strong as a gymnast. He is also viewed as effeminate by some of the football players, which seems like an underlying reason he is targeted after participating in a weight room contest in which he and his teammate, Danny Meehan, out-perform the football players in a feat of strength. Ronnie and Danny are chosen by the football players to represent the gymnastics team in the contest because they are the "smallest on the team, and, [the football players assumed] the weakest" (Cohen, 2011, p. 42). Immediately after the contest, two football players physically assault Ronnie and Danny. The first, Tom Jankowski, pulls Danny away, grabs him around the neck, and tells him that he and his "little pussy friends are dead. You hear me? Dead. We are gonna bury you" (p. 48). The second, Todd Pullman, twists Ronnie's arm violently behind his back. These are the same football players that ultimately rape Ronnie.

Josh, at the time of his abuse as a middle school student, is described as mature for his age. He is also proud of his "A Grade" streak in school and is particularly adept at math and statistics, often using baseball stats to explain what is happening in his life. These characteristics are the reasons why his middle school history teacher, Eve Sherman, initially noticed him. For example, on the way home from the first parent-teacher conference of the school year, his mother reports that Eve spoke about Josh in this way:

> She said that you're her best student, but was worried at first because you look so much older and more mature than most of the other kids. She thought you had been held back a year and she couldn't figure out why you were in the advanced class. So she was relieved when you turned out to be a smart kid. (Lyga, 2007, p. 115)

Eve also called Josh her "little historian" (p. 115) during that parent-teacher conference and uses Josh's school success as a way to convince his parents to be alone with her after school and, eventually, at her apartment, as a participant in her supposed graduate school research project. These were early steps in Eve's plan to groom Josh into accepting her sexual advances.

Portrayals of Victimhood

The selected novels frame living as a victim of sexual violence as a shameful experience for male youth-athletes. The shame is too much to bear for some of these characters. In *Swagger*, readers can infer Levi's shame from his posture, his denial, and his refusal to speak out. After the first instance of Coach Hartwell's abuse, Levi's "shoulders were slumped and his head was down" (Deuker, 2013, p. 162), illustrating how shame takes a physical toll. Later, when Jonas asks Levi what troubles him, he offers a swift denial, as if there is shame in acknowledging that he has been subject to sexual abuse: "Nothing's wrong, Jonas" (p. 176). Once Jonas learns of the sexual abuse his friend has suffered, Levi refuses to talk further, declaring, "I'm not telling anybody else. I'm never telling anybody else" (p. 219). Ultimately, Levi's shame is so great that, after confirming Jonas's intent to speak to authorities on his behalf, he is found dead, a victim of the elements at Kachess Lake, a secluded location in the wilderness area outside his city. Given Levi's commitment to wilderness survival established earlier in the novel (p. 75), readers can conclude he died by suicide, an effort to halt the shame associated with suffering sexual abuse.

Leverage, too, presents a victim of sexual violence whose intense feelings of shame precede suicide. Days after enduring a violent rape, Ronnie is found dead in a bathtub (Cohen, 2011, p. 200). His death comes after he describes for Danny the perceived permanence of his agony: "I feel…I can't wash it off…. it's like when you're…. like a poison…need to boil it away" (p. 189). When Danny conveys difficulty comprehending what he just heard, Ronnie explains further, "…washing doesn't help…. It's *inside!*" (p. 189, italics in original). Ronnie's extreme feelings of shame are seemingly amplified by the problematic advice he receives from another teammate, Bruce Nguyen, who recommends that Ronnie "act like nothing happened" (p. 189). To make matters worse, Danny endorses Bruce's poor counsel: "Look, Ronnie, take Bruce's advice. Nothing happened" (p. 189). And when Ronnie attempts to rebut that recommendation, Danny offers a final directive: "Stop it. Just stop it. Get over it" (p. 190). Unable to "act like nothing happened" and simply "get over" the violent rape he suffered, Ronnie dies by suicide.

Boy Toy also depicts living as a victim of sexual violence as a shameful experience, though without fatal consequences. For Josh, his shame is tied to an erroneous belief that he seduced Eve five years prior. Informed by a headline quoting an attorney who labeled the abuse a "Sin of Opportunity" (Lyga, 2007, p. 397), Josh fails to believe his therapist and his parents, who have insisted for years that he, a child, was not responsible for Eve's actions but, rather, that he was subjected to her abuse. Josh's overwhelming feelings of shame are grounded in the false belief that he is culpable and, subsequently, that he is a pariah at school, where teachers fear him and fret "they'll catch the molester virus" (p. 30). It is not until Josh confronts Eve that he comes to understand how she manipulated him from the start, grooming him by providing video games, sharing wine, and generally treating him like an adult (pp. 398-399). Though not leading to suicide, the shame Josh feels from Eve's sexual abuse negatively affects his life for years.

In addition to being distinguished by feelings of shame, portrayals of victimhood in these stories are also marked by the perpetuation of violence. That is, two of the male youth-athletes who suffer sexual abuse exhibit physically violent behavior against others. For example, in *Boy Toy*, Josh punches his varsity baseball coach, Mr. Kaltenbach, for uttering an insult related to the sexual abuse Eve inflicted upon him years prior (Lyga, 2007, pp. 15-16), and he recalls the time he landed multiple punches on a schoolmate who incidentally bumped into him one day after Eve's trial (p. 337). Though the degree of provocation for each attack varies, such violence is rooted in Josh's history as a victim of sexual abuse. Likewise, Levi, a victim in *Swagger*, grows violent in relation to Coach Hartwell's sexual abuse. For instance, he becomes angry during the state basketball tournament, commits a brutal foul, and has to be dragged away from the court (Deuker, 2013, p. 204). Jonas's mother recognizes Levi's atypical behavior as symptomatic of greater problems: "What happened with Levi tonight? I didn't know he had such a temper.... It's never been part of Levi's game. Is something wrong?" (p. 205). For these characters, lashing out violently is an apparent symptom of sexual abuse.

Discussion

As we established in the introduction, in the U.S., sexual violence is more commonly perpetrated against juvenile girls than juvenile boys by a wide margin (RAINN, 2023b). Any discussion of the victimization of male youth—in the world or on the page—must be considered within this larger context. And yet, as noted previously, boys do constitute approximately 20% of the juvenile victims of sexual violence in the U.S. (RAINN, 2023b), so the victimization of juvenile boys cannot be ignored. The authors of *Swagger*, *Leverage*, and *Boy Toy* recognize as much, for they tackle such victimization head on with depictions of male youth-athletes who are subject to sexual violence, often with fatal consequences. In that way, these stories complement the various works of sports-related YAL that depict male youth-athletes as perpetrators of sexual violence against young women, including the novels Boehm and colleagues (2020) examined.

With plots that are driven by acts of sexual violence perpetrated against male youth-athletes, *Swagger*, *Leverage*, and *Boy Toy* are valuable works of sports-related YAL because they are stories that might otherwise go untold, because they shine a light on matters many people opt to avoid. These novels convey the gravity of sexual violence through realistic portrayals of male youth-athletes who are hurt by people in their orbit, which reflects what is known about the preponderance of sexual violence against children and teenagers being committed by someone they know (RAINN, 2023a). Moreover, as a set, these novels accurately communicate that perpetrators of sexual violence against male youth-athletes can take different forms: They are teachers, coaches, and fellow athletes; men and women; trusted adults and antagonistic peers. And with victims that range from the diminutive Ronnie Gunderson to the sizable Levi Rawdon, these novels reflect the fact that one's stature is not a surefire guard against sexual violence being perpetrated against them.

In two of the three selected novels a male youth-athlete is so overwhelmed by feelings of shame that he loses his life to suicide. Therefore, these particular characters are not "survivors" by RAINN's (n.d.) definition, which refers to "someone who has gone through the recovery process." For Ronnie Gunderson and Levi Rawdon, there is no recovery. While this pattern does underscore the grave nature of sexual violence, it does not offer a particularly hopeful message of survival for young readers. The emphasis on suicide as a solution to dealing with such trauma is troubling, given that some young readers are sure to recognize aspects of their own lives and experiences (i.e., sexual abuse or sexual assault) depicted in these stories. For these readers in particular, more stories that accurately convey the gravity of sexual violence while also offering hope for survival—for recovery—may be beneficial.

We do believe that these three novels hold promise for talking about sexual violence with youth because they present authentic plots about genuine characters. However, we encourage teachers to define related terminology prior to teaching any story that involves sexual violence. This step ensures that everyone has the same understanding about such terms and when to use different terms based on the actual incident or situation. Particularly, we suggest reviewing the nuance in the denotative and connotative meanings of "victim" and "survivor" by multiple resources and the disparate behaviors of harassment, grooming, exploitation, and rape. We recommend reviewing the definitions of these terms, along with other resources, provided by RAINN (n.d.) and the Stop Sexual Assault in Schools (n.d.) organization. We also suggest discussing the relationship between consent and positions of power, particularly if teaching stories like *Swagger* or *Boy Toy*, both of which involve adults abusing their power as trusted figures in youths' lives.

In this vein, *Swagger* and *Boy Toy* could be used to talk about ways individuals use their position to take advantage of others. Both Coach Hartwell and Eve are adults who hold power over Levi and Josh, respectively, and use that power to create situations in which they can be alone with them. Coach Hartwell takes on

Levi as a tutee to help him with his academics, and Eve finds reasons for Josh to visit her apartment under the guise of contributing to her graduate thesis. These stories could be used to show younger readers how to recognize such situations. As well, all three of these stories illustrate the effects of sexual violence on the demeanor and actions of the victims, so teachers could talk about looking for signs of distress in their friends and family. Teachers would also want to identify safer actions youth could take if they see such signs. Particularly, we suggest talking about the roles bystanders can take to help their friends and family, such as speaking with a trusted adult about any concerns they might have, rather than attempting to intervene on their own.

In addition to reviewing pertinent terminology, we also suggest that teachers share statistics from RAINN and UNESCO about sexual harassment and sexual abuse, prior to teaching any of these novels. Doing so stands to establish the importance of thinking and talking about this issue in an ELA setting. Further, discussing victim blaming and rape myth acceptance with secondary-aged readers would be an essential step to help frame their perspectives about the characters' experiences and their subsequent responses to the stories. This might involve asking students to review the Illinois Rape Myth Acceptance Scale (Thelan & Meadows, 2021) and/or asking students to complete the survey and report out the results anonymously for class discussion. Finally, we suggest that teachers talk about their intention to teach such stories with their administration and with their students' guardians to protect themselves and their students.

Conclusion

According to RAINN (2023b), only about 30% of sexual assaults are reported to the police, with only about 20% of college-aged women reporting. Due to additional stigmas and even fewer resources, the percentage of men who report is most likely significantly lower and, until the 1990s and 2000s, most legal definitions of rape were only defined as a male assaulting a female or child (see Thomas & Kopel, 2023, for a complete review of the literature on male victims of sexual violence). It is imperative that young people understand that sexual violence can be perpetrated by both males and females and upon both males and females. Reading and discussing young adult stories like the three we have explored in this chapter is one way to further this understanding among secondary-aged youth.

References

Adams, B. (2020). "I didn't feel confident talking about this issue…but I knew I could talk about a book": Using young adult literature to make sense of #metoo. *Journal of Literacy Research*, 52(2), 209–230.

Boehm, S., Colantonio-Yurko, K., Olmstead, K., & Miller, H. C. (2020). Athlete as agitator, assaulter, and armor: Sports, identity, and sexual assault in young adult literature. *Study and Scrutiny: Research on Young Adult Literature, 4*(2), 31-56.

Bruner, B. (2023, Nov 21). Lawsuit accuses Gallia County coach, ex-wife of sexually abusing athletes for 15 years. *The Columbus Dispatch.* https://www.dispatch.com/story/news/courts/2023/11/20/lawsuit-gallia-county-coach-wife-years-sexual-abuse-paige-huck-river-valley-high-school-matt-huck/71656323007/

Charles, A. (2019). Sexual assault and its impact on young adult literature. *Criterion: A Journal of Literary Criticism, 12*(2), 97-103.

Cleveland, E., & Durand, S. (2014). Critical representations of sexual assault in young adult literature. *The Looking Glass: New Perspectives on Children's Literature, 17*(3). https://ojs.latrobe.edu.au/ojs/index.php/tlg/article/view/545

Cohen, J. (2011). *Leverage.* Dutton Books.

Colantonio-Yurko, K. C., Miller, H. C., & Cheveallier, J. (2018). "But she didn't scream": Teaching about sexual assault in young adult literature. *Journal of Language & Literacy Education, 14*(1), 1-16.

Deuker, C. (2013). *Swagger.* Houghton Mifflin.

Jurado, A. (2023, Sep 27). SC school district pays six-figure settlement in locker room sexual assault lawsuit. *The State.*

Konigsberg, B. (2019). *The music of what happens.* Arthur A. Levine Books.

Lyga, B. (2007). *Boy toy.* Houghton Mifflin.
https://www.thestate.com/news/local/education/article279825004.html

Malo-Juvera, V. (2014). *Speak:* The effect of literacy instruction on adolescents' rape myth acceptance. *Research in the Teaching of English, 48*(4), 407-427.

Miller, H. C., Boehm, S., Colantonio-Yurko, K., & Adams, B. (2022). Himpathy, herasure, and down girl moves: A critical content analysis of sexual assault in young adult literature. *Journal of Literacy Research, 54*(3), 298–321.

Prasad, A. (2002). The contest over meaning: Hermeneutics as an interpretive methodology for understanding texts. *Organizational Research Methods, 5*(1), 12-33.

Rape, Abuse & Incest National Network (RAINN). (2023a). *Children and teens: Statistics.* https://www.rainn.org/statistics/children-and-teens

Rape, Abuse & Incest National Network (RAINN). (2023b). *Victims of sexual violence: Statistics.* https://www.rainn.org/statistics/victims-sexual-violence

Rape, Abuse & Incest National Network (RAINN). (n.d.). *Key terms and phrases.* https://www.rainn.org/articles/key-terms-and-phrases

Reid, S. M. (2023, Aug 31). Former El Segundo High water polo players allege sexual abuse by ex-coach George Harris. *Daily Breeze.* https://www.dailybreeze

.com/2023/08/31/former-el-segundo-high-water-polo-players-allege-sexual-abuse-by-ex-coach-george-harris/

Schilken, C. (2024, Feb 29). Ex-NFL player alleges sexual abuse by Colton High trainer who was coach's daughter. *Los Angeles Times.* https://www.latimes.com/california/story/2024-02-29/shareece-wright-sexual-abuse-lawsuit-colton-high-school-district-tiffany-strauss-gordon

Schwandt, T. A. (2015). *The SAGE dictionary of qualitative inquiry* (4th ed.). SAGE.

Stop Sexual Assault in Schools. (n.d.). https://stopsexualassaultinschools.org/

Thelan, A. R., & Meadows, E. A. (2021). The Illinois rape myth acceptance scale—subtle version: Using an adapted measure to understand the declining rates of rape myth acceptance. *Journal of Interpersonal Violence, 37*(19–20), NP17807–NP17833.

Thomas, J. C., & Kopel, J. (2023). Male victims of sexual assault: A review of the literature. *Behavioral Sciences, 13*(4), 304-326.

United Nations Educational, Scientific and Cultural Organization (UNESCO). (2023). *Tackling violence against women and girls in sport: A handbook for policy makers and sports practitioners.* https://www.unwomen.org/sites/default/files/2023-07/3343_unwomen_unesco_vawg_handbook_6a_singlepage.pdf

III. Critical Understandings, Teaching, and Application

Disrupting Rape Myths and Objective Violence through Graphic Novels: A Critical Literacy Approach to Educating Emergent Bilingual Youth

Jie Y. Park, Clark University

While designed to mitigate sexual violence, comprehensive sex education and antirape programs are often not designed for immigrant youth who are recent arrivals to the U.S. That is, when offered, the programs do not include lessons that are culturally relevant and linguistically accessible to recent arrival youth who are emergent bilinguals (Manduley et al., 2018). In this chapter recent arrivals refer to youth who were born outside of the U.S. and spent at least two-thirds of their lives in their country of origin (Suárez-Orozco et al., 2008). A heterogeneous group, the majority come from Latin America, Asia, and the Afro-Caribbean basin (Garcia & Kleifgen, 2018). They typically enter the U.S. at the secondary level of schooling and take classes in English as a Second Language (ESL). The emergent bilinguals in this chapter attended a school that did not offer comprehensive sex education or anti-rape education. Instead, much of their education about, and inquiry into, sexuality and sexual violence occurred in their ESL classes. Drawing on ethnographic data collected in a high-school ESL class, this chapter offers two practices—critical literacy pedagogy and the use of graphic novels—that support immigrant youth to challenge representations of sexual violence and interrogate the role of authors, texts, and discourses in reinforcing (or disrupting) objective violence. Graphic novels in the classroom can foster emergent bilinguals' critical stance (Colantonio-Yurko et al., 2022). This is because it is easier for emergent bilinguals to understand that the visual images in graphic novels are representations, created by a human being with a particular point of view and set of beliefs (Park, 2016).

Theoretical Frameworks

The chapter posits that emergent bilinguals, through critical literacy pedagogy, can interrogate what critical theorist Slavoj Žižek referred to as objective violence. In *Violence: Six Sideways Reflections*, Žižek (2008) differentiates objective violence from subjective violence, noting that subjective violence involves a subject or "clearly identifiable agent" (p. 1) who is the perpetrator. Subjective violence is focused on the individual and at the interpersonal-level. Objective violence, however, is carried out in language and discourses (Anwaruddin, 2016;

Žižek, 2008). Offering the example of anti-Semitic pogroms, Žižek in a later piece (2016) noted that anti-Semites are provoked by the "image/figure of the 'Jew' which... overdetermines the way [they] experience real Jews themselves and, furthermore, it affects the way Jews experience themselves" (p.2). In other words, objective violence is carried out discursively and normalized through cultural models, symbols, images, and interpretive frames.

I suggest that objective violence is useful in sexual violence education because it goes beyond the single "bad" actor, and instead highlights the discursive and cultural production of rape culture, which includes messages about consent, violence, and recognizability. Addressing sexual violence, Anwaruddin (2016) who also cites Žižek's concept of objective violence, identifies a dominant frame which blames victim-survivors of sexual assault for their dress and/or behavior. This frame also operates to render certain individuals' lives as "recognizable" while other lives (i.e., Black and brown women or trans folx) are not fully recognizable, meaning that their "suffering and loss do not qualify as grievable" (Anwaruddin, p. 263). Objective violence is more challenging to address than subjective violence because it is in our everyday discourses and cultural productions, and therefore "in the air." Take as an example, the objective violence in health education textbooks (Clonan-Roy et al., 2021). A content analysis of 16 health education textbooks revealed that in most textbooks, there was a "discourse of violence, victimization, and individual morality... that emphasized boys as aggressors and initiators, and girls as gatekeepers and resistors" (Clonan-Roy et al., p. 242).

Disrupting objective violence is not just an interpretive or discursive exercise. In fact, scholars like Anwaruddin (2016) argue that in order to prevent subjective violence, we have to dismantle objective violence. Put differently, "Every world is sustained by language, and every 'spoken' language sustains a world" (Žižek, 2016, p. 10). Language does not just serve practical, social, or even aesthetic functions, but ideological and world-building functions as well (Alim, 2010). If we are, as Žižek claims, caught in language, how can people step outside of language in order to critique and transform it?

One possible solution to dismantling objective violence is through critical literacy pedagogy (see Young, 2000; 2001, for a similar argument about critical literacy pedagogy in deconstructing dominant gender ideologies). Acknowledging that critical literacy does not have a single definition, I adopt in my own work the understanding of critical literacy as the capacity to interrogate the word and world (Freire, 1987). This can be done through questioning who wrote the text (text, broadly defined, to include cultural and institutional productions), for whom, in what context, and for whose interests (Luke & Freebody, 1997). According to critical literacy, our ways of meaning-making and meaning-sharing are never neutral, but entangled in power relationships. Critical literacy pedagogy, therefore, refers to an approach to education that highlights the interconnectedness of ideology, power, culture, and language. At its core, critical literacy pedagogy is about interrogating what seems logical, natural, and commonsensical, and exposing the ways in which they are ideologically motivated and discursively constructed (Luke, 2018). To put it differently, in critical literacy pedagogy students come to question language and texts "in relationship to their effects in the world – the interests that are served" (Janks et al., 2013, p. 83). Questioning texts and discourses (and the interests they serve) cannot be done through the banking model where the teacher decides on and transmits the content. Instead, critical literacy pedagogy relies on dialogue or dialogic practices, in which students grapple with their own observations of and questions about the social world.

While critical literacy is not just a set of strategies (Luke, 2004; 2018), a review of critical literacy classrooms identified six common pedagogical practices: (1) reading supplementary texts, (2) reading multiple texts, (3) reading from a resistant perspective, (4) producing counter-texts, (5) conducting student-choice research projects, and (6) taking social action (Behrman, 2006). While Behrman's review covers a limited time period between 1999 and 2003, their meta-analysis aligns with more contemporary descriptions of critical literacy classrooms in which teachers use diverse literature (Colantonio-Yurko et al., 2022, Low et al., 2021), and apply dialogue to disrupt what appears natural, universal or commonplace (Anwaruddin, 2016; Ayers, 2019). In classrooms with emergent bilinguals, critical literacy education centers the youths' languages, identities, and experiences as sources of knowledge; decenters English as the sole language of teaching and learning; emphasizes participation in meaningful intellectual and social activities; theorizes language and literacy as political and ideological constructs; and treats language and literacy as resources by which we not only read the word and world, but transform them (Park, 2023).

Context and Methodology

The emergent bilingual youths in this chapter attended New Visions (a pseudonym), a grade 7-12 school where over 80 percent of its 550 students speak a language other than English at home and 90 percent receive free and reduced-priced lunch. While the majority of emergent bilinguals come from the Dominican Republic, El Salvador, Honduras, and Guatemala, they also come from Nepal, Haiti, and Ghana. In the state where the research took place, anti-rape education programs are not mandated. At the time when I was working with the emergent bilingual youth and their ESL teacher, the school provided a two-week long curriculum on health and human anatomy, which covered reproduction, but not rape prevention, consent, or body boundaries.

As for my positionality, I am a 1.5 generation immigrant, Korean American cis woman. In 2014, I began a seven-year, collaborative research partnership with three ESL teachers at New Visions, bringing not only my lived experiences as a former ELA and ESL educator, but my commitment to designing linguistically and culturally sustaining classrooms for emergent bilinguals (Paris & Alim, 2017). I worked with Lori and her two colleagues in the ESL department to document and make sense of their daily work, engaging in practitioner inquiry (Cochran-Smith & Lytle, 2009). As part of our research partnership, I audio-recorded discussions in the ESL classrooms, conducted interviews with emergent bilingual youth, took fieldnotes, and collected student work and other artifacts. It is important to state that I am not writing this as a scholar of youth sexuality or sexuality education. In terms of my scholarly identity, I see my research as situated at the intersection of critical literacies, multiliteracies, and multilingualism as they are practiced and negotiated by immigrant-origin youth and classroom teachers.

A white monolingual woman in her late 40s, Lori played a central role in facilitating emergent bilinguals' academic and social transitions in school. She leveraged diverse literature of different genres, including graphic novels and young adult fiction. For the purposes of this chapter, I highlight data from a unit Lori taught on *The League of Extraordinary Gentlemen*, a graphic novel by Alan Moore and Kevin O'Neill. Twenty-one students participated in the graphic novel curriculum over six and a half weeks. The data include transcripts of classroom interactions and discussions, teacher artifacts (e.g., lesson plans), and student work. The graphic novel depicts several instances of rape and sexual assault, which the youth picked up on and wrestled with, both in their class discussions and written work.

To make sense of the data, I first examined the youths' comments about subjective and objective violence (in writing and discussion). From this step in the analysis process, I learned that students' initial comments about sexual violence, prompted by images in the graphic novel, focused mostly on subjective violence, specifically the individuals involved in the violent act (as a perpetrator or victim-survivor) – for example, the way that the perpetrator or victim-survivor looked. In this step, I also learned that the youth tended to describe women in the graphic novel, many who are victim-survivors of sexual violence, in the passive voice ("She almost got raped"). There were many instances when students did not even name the assailant in the text.

However, the youths' comments, many which were about subjective violence, were embedded in, and invoked various discourses about sex and sexual violence.

That is, their discourses were an example of objective violence. To unpack the youths' relationship to these discourses, I used a discourse analytic approach, which assumes that language is not only contextual and situated, but also emerges from, invokes, and reinforces certain "cultural models", defined as:

> '[S]torylines', families of connected images (like a mental movie), or (informal) 'theories' shared by people belonging to specific social or cultural groups. Cultural models 'explain', relative to the standards of the group (though often at a fairly taken-for-granted and unconscious level), the sorts of situated meanings that people tend to assemble for their words and phrases. (Gee, 2004, p. 20)

Cultural models are images, narratives, or worldviews that not only explain, but uphold what is seen as 'appropriate,' 'normal' or 'good' by a specific social or cultural group. Cultural models, therefore, are tied to a speaker/writer's social identities or group memberships. For example, while not exclusive to male-identifying youth, more young men than young women in Lori's class expressed that some rape victim-survivors (always women or girls, in their comments) are less sympathetic because of their dress, behavior, or profession. This idea is part of the dominant cultural model or rape culture that dictates that "men are active while women are passive... men have a right to sexual intercourse... [and] there are blurred lines around consent" (Phipps et al., 2018, p. 1). In the rest of the chapter, I offer empirical accounts of emergent bilingual youth coming to grapple with objective violence, highlighting not only their critical capacities, but the pedagogical practices that enable them.

Findings: A Youth-Led Inquiry into Sexual Violence

In this section, I begin by sharing classroom discussions about gender and sexual violence, followed by a description of the final project, which involved a jury trial. I call attention to specific critical literacy practices and the learning they engendered in students. Throughout this section, I use language that upholds the female/male binary. The graphic novel itself upheld the female/male binary, and the emergent bilingual youths in the ESL class also identified themselves and others (including those in the graphic novel) through a binary lens. While I recognize that this binary is exclusionary (and it is not my intent to use harmful and exclusionary language), I chose to keep the youths' characterizations about themselves, each other, and the literary characters.

Classroom Discussions about Gender and Sexual Violence

Lori did not set out to teach about rape and rape culture in *The League of Extraordinary Gentlemen*. Instead, she chose the text for its connections to required texts in the ELA curriculum, including Bram Stoker's *Dracula* and HG

Well's *Invisible Man*. As previously noted, the graphic novel contains scenes of sexual violence. The first scene takes place in Egypt where Mina Murray, one of the main characters and the only female character, is assaulted by local men. What follows is an exchange between the youth (all pseudonyms) about several panels depicting the assault:

> *Johnny:* Oh. She almost got raped.
> *Ana:* She actually did got raped.
> *Martin:* She almost did.
> *Chris:* What page is that?
> *Carlos:* Was she a thot?
> *Lori (T):* A thot?
> *Johnny:* A girl, a female that don't treat themselves like women supposed to treat themselves.
> *Ana:* Yea. they use their body for attention.
> *Martin:* Attention.

In this instance, the youth began the discussion with a focus on Mina Murray as a subject, and whether she was "actually" or "almost" raped. The first part of the discussion emphasized subjective violence. But when Carlos wondered whether Mina Murray was a thot, he surfaced deeply-ingrained cultural models about gender and violence – a hegemonic belief that sexual violence against women is somehow connected to their demeanor or dress. Carlos was not the only one to invoke this cultural model, with Johnny and Ana also adding to the definition of "thot."

In the youths' responses to the graphic novel, they often positioned women as passive victims of assault, not even naming the perpetrator. In a different scene that portrays rape at an all-girls' school, the youth engaged in this conversation:

> *Barry:* Girls is raped.
> *Carlos:* And they don't know who.
> *Barry:* Raped by the Invisible Man.
> *Lori (T):* Why is Alan Moore putting stuff like this in?

Instead of stating that the Invisible Man rapes the girls, the youth often talked about rape as something that happens to girls or women. As Barry noted, the girls cannot even see who is raping them. In the graphic novel, one of the female students at the school states, "A holy spirit just sorta entered into me." Making the rapist literally invisible is part of a discourse in which the "criminality of rape is rhetorically and grammatically erased" (Makoni, 2011, p. 354).

However, Lori's question of why Alan Moore would include such scenes prompted youth to grapple with the representations of rape and the discourses of gender and violence in the text (i.e., objective violence). In writing about Alan Moore's views on women and power, the youth wrote comments such as "The way Alan Moore writes things and describes things are perverted and somewhat stereotypical, like the way he wrote the guys from Cairo;" and "He [Moore] thinks of women, he thinks of all women as they not important. They're not great." They also wrote "He thinks that other women are like flirty kinds of women;" and asked "That picture is representing how women should act or what?"

In their comments, Lori and I saw the emergent bilingual youths' critical capacities. The comments not only problematized "stereotypical" discourses, but challenged Moore's depiction of Arab men assaulting a white woman, who is eventually rescued by a white man. In the second comment, the youth called out the gender hierarchy in the graphic novel, inferring that Moore himself thinks that women are not important or worthy. But it was the last comment that really made us pause: The student wondered whether depictions of sexual violence and the positioning of women (as docile and naive, or as promiscuous) represented a normative view of the world – that is, the way women *should* act – and why Alan Moore would include such representations.

The Final Project: Putting Alan Moore on Trial

Throughout the graphic novel unit, Lori and I supported the emergent bilingual youth to engage in critical analysis at two levels. The first level was their own beliefs about rape and instances in which they expressed misogynistic and dangerous discourses. This was, for example, when Eric stated that some girls/women enjoy rape or when Mauricio noted, "Rape exists everywhere. The way they dress make you want to rape them." Rather than tell the youth that they were wrong, we questioned where their beliefs came from and what alternatives they could imagine. The second level of analysis was Alan Moore's beliefs about rape, the discourses represented in the graphic novel, and the graphic novel's relationship to objective violence. The youth wanted to know – by writing about rape, was Alan Moore guilty of normalizing objective violence or was he trying to deconstruct it?

Given the two levels of critical analysis, Lori and I decided that the final project would be a jury trial – where students would have to assume the perspectives of the characters in the graphic novel and use textual evidence and knowledge about Alan Moore to engage with the various discourses in the text. Instead of adjudicating students' personal beliefs about sexual violence, Lori put Alan Moore and the discourses of the graphic novel on trial. Specifically, Lori asked students to bring forward a specific charge against Alan Moore. At that time, we did not have the language to describe objective and subjective violence. But the youth voted to charge Alan Moore with sexism. They each chose a role to play in the jury trial: attorney (prosecution or defense); character witness; or jury member. Lori played the judge and I was the court reporter/transcriber.

Preparing emergent bilingual youth for the trial, Lori created scaffolds and established clear expectations and guidelines. She spent the first few days helping the entire class build relevant background knowledge on jury trials in the U.S. In addition to showing clips from the television series like *How to Get Away with Murder* and *Law and Order*, Lori created written handouts explaining the responsibilities of each role (witness, attorney, jury). For youth playing a character witness, Lori offered information about each character: Captain Nemo, Mina Murray, Invisible Man, and Dr. Jekyll/Mr. Hyde. She offered links to online sources (and encouraged youth to find online sources in languages they preferred). For youth playing the prosecution or defense attorney, she directed them to online resources, such as YouTube videos of Alan Moore discussing *The League of Extraordinary Gentlemen* and his philosophy as an artist. In addition to providing resources for each role, Lori assigned daily tasks for students to complete and conferenced with them about their progress. Lori encouraged emergent bilinguals to utilize tools like Google Translate and recruit their entire linguistic repertoire (e.g., writing a draft of the opening statement in Spanish, giving jury testimony in Spanish) (Garcia et al., 2017).

During the trial, students wrestled with the objective violence in the graphic novel, carried out through visual images as well as its written language/discourses. The students cited the invisibility of women as an instance of objective violence – although they did not use the term, objective violence. They critiqued how women are less prominent in the graphic novel, with only one female member in the league of "extraordinary gentlemen." Josue, a recent arrival from the Dominican Republic, pointed out that Mina Murray, unlike the men, did not have any special powers. While there had been plenty of talk about the over-representation of female sex workers during the trial, Josue was the first to argue (in Spanish) that while the men in the graphic novel held special powers or positions of leadership, Mina Murray had neither. Cleo, playing the character witness of Mina Murray, also testified that Alan Moore was guilty of sexism. In addition to the scenes of sexual violence, Cleo (as Mina Murray) presented an analysis of power. Describing the role of women in the graphic novel and in general, she noted, "You know we don't rule the society. Society rules us. I think society rules us. We don't rule it." Here, Cleo suggested the connection between gender oppression and violence.

Except Mina Murray, many women in the graphic novel are faceless, nameless, and/or voiceless. This is a form of objective violence (Anwaruddin, 2016). But did depicting women in such a way make Alan Moore sexist? Different parts of the trial suggested that this was a complicated and epistemically rich question for the youth. In her opening statement, Josie, a young woman from Puerto Rico, stated that Alan Moore normalizes misogyny. Playing the court reporter, I transcribed the statement:

> Hi, good morning ladies and gentlemen of the jury. I have come here today to prove to you that Alan Moore is sexist. I have many witnesses that will testify and support this. You will see evidence that Alan Moore is sexist. On October 26, 2000, Alan Moore published *The League of Extraordinary Gentlemen*. He showed women as prostitute and sex objects. With this, he shows that men are more superior than women. This shows that Alan Moore believe that men are superior. Alan Moore will… say that one reason he start writing this book is because he wants to prove to the people that violation of women exists in society. I have five witnesses that will testify that Alan Moore does believe women are lower than men, and that he is making people think that this is ok. Thank you.

During witness testimonies, Barry, a youth from the Dominican Republic, played Alan Moore. While on the stand as a witness for the defense, he argued that he (as Alan Moore) was not sexist. In fact, Alan Moore is a champion of women because he brings awareness to an underrepresented issue: sexual violence against women. Martin played the defense attorney for Alan Moore.

Martin: What do you think of women?
Barry: I have two daughters which I love and a wife.
Martin: Why did you illustrate, why did you write about women and rape?
Barry: I wanted to take a moment to represent sexual violence even though it's a really bad thing. I think it's something that happens and we have to talk about it. Open up society into what sexual violence is. It [sexual violence] is focused on my work because I wanted to talk about it. I wanted to tell people. Something happened to society, and I wanted to talk about it.
Martin: What do you think about sexual abuse?
Barry: Sexual abuse is really bad thing that needs to be talked about.
Martin: Thank you.

Barry-as-Alan Moore stated that while sexual violence is prominent in the graphic novel, Moore does not approve of or agree with sexual violence. In fact, Barry argued that Moore's intention was to prompt society to dialogue about sexual violence against women. Barry's theory of change was that the more people talked about sexual violence, the more we could combat it.

Discussion: Putting Discourses of Sexual Violence on Trial

Throughout the trial, emergent bilingual youth grappled with ideological, philosophical, and ethical questions: What are the discourses of gender and sexual violence in the graphic novel? Is it sexist to represent a sexist world? When an artist depicts rape, what (if anything) can or should we infer about the artist's own worldviews? What moral or ethical responsibilities do artists have? The youth-as-jury members were unsure of their stance and raised more questions than they had definitive answers. They wondered: What is the definition of sexism? Is the definition of sexism different now than it was at the time in the graphic novel? Does that matter? Youth in the jury also brought up points that the attorneys did not even acknowledge – for instance, that Alan Moore most likely had male readers in mind when creating the graphic novel. The intended audience could have shaped his decisions as an artist.

Instead of directly putting the students' beliefs and worldviews on trial, Lori put Alan Moore and the discourses of gender and sexual violence on trial. And while ostensibly about Alan Moore, the trial prompted emergent bilingual youth to surface and re-examine *different* cultural models about gender, sex, and sexual violence. Our goal was not to arrive at a judgment about them or even about Alan Moore, but invite critical literacy practices – engaging with forms of objective violence that seem "normal" or "commonplace," exploring the connection between power, representation, and social worlds, and coming to see texts as non-neutral and political (Janks et al., 2013).

From participating in the trial, emergent bilingual youth came to understand that how we represent (or communicate about) acts of sexual violence, whether visually and/or through words, matters. In other words, representations contain not only scenes of events and people, but uphold belief systems associated with rape. What belief system is invoked when the rape scene focuses on the woman's dress? The youth agreed that how a graphic novelist portrays women can influence the readers' beliefs about sexual violence. A youth on the jury noted, "Rape is not the same thing as prostitution. But Alan Moore shows both in the book." Students also realized that the graphic novelist's positionality and social identities matter. This was made evident when they wondered whether a woman would have created the graphic novel in the same way as Alan Moore, or the connection between Alan Moore's whiteness and his depiction of Chinese and Arab men as "cruel" or "dirty."

Also important to note, by grappling with the objective violence in the graphic novel, some youth began to shift their own discourses. Barry, for example, said that having to play Alan Moore and defend Alan Moore's choices as a graphic novelist challenged his own views. Initially he believed that Moore should not have included scenes of rape. But he shifted his views over the course of the trial, acknowledging the importance of openly naming social problems as a prerequisite to change.

A final point, the youth expressed that while individual beliefs about gender and rape can change, the power structures and gender hierarchy very much remain. While they did not offer ideas about shifting or dismantling gender hierarchies, they wondered about the role of literature and texts more broadly in remaking the social world.

Implications for Practice

Enabled by the graphic novel and critical literacy pedagogy, emergent bilingual youth in Lori's ESL class came to interrogate objective violence. While some educators believe that critical literacy is "not for all learners" (Ralfe, 2009), critical literacy is possible with emergent bilinguals who are still learning to decode and comprehend written English. Ralfe (2009) noted: "Without comprehension, critical interrogation of texts is impossible" (p. 318). But with a critical literacy pedagogy that decenters the written word in favor of a more expansive notion of texts (e.g., graphic novels), and that actively recruits the assets of emergent bilinguals (e.g., youths' visual literacies and stance of questioning what is "normal"), emergent bilinguals who are still learning to "read the word" are capable of sophisticated discourse analysis and critique.

Anwaruddin (2016) offers four dimensions of critical literacy pedagogy: 1) disrupting the commonplace; 2) interrogating multiple viewpoints; 3) focusing on sociopolitical issues and their connection to language; and 4) taking action for social justice. These four dimensions are similar to the critical literacy practices, as reviewed by Behrman (2006). But neither Anwaruddin nor Behrman explicitly address what it means to design educational spaces for emergent bilingual youth. This oversight works against the efforts of ESL and language educators in supporting emergent bilinguals as they navigate a new school system and country. Furthermore, discussions about sex and sexual violence can (and do) happen inside ESL classrooms, outside of mandated health or sex education programs. Therefore, in this last part, I address ESL and language educators as well as health educators and offer a set of pedagogical considerations when educating emergent bilinguals. The ideas below are informed by what I learned in Lori's class, from Lori and the emergent bilingual youth themselves:

Consideration 1

During the jury trial, emergent bilingual youths used multiple languages. Even if Lori could not understand what students were saying, she presumed their intelligence and meaning-making capacities. For example, Josue used mostly Spanish during the jury trial, but asked Barry, a classmate, to act as the court translator. Josie wrote her opening statement in Spanish before translating it into English. This suggests that critical literacy education has to be multilingual. Rather than an exclusive focus on English (i.e., using English to teach English), a multilingual orientation sees multilingualism as a normal condition and resource for teaching and learning. It also conceptualizes learning as a collaborative, multilingual activity (Meier, 2017). Multilingual orientation challenges linguistic descriptors like "standard" or "appropriate" and recognizes the interconnectedness of race, ethnicity, language, and power (Baker-Bell, 2020; Flores & Rosa, 2015).

Consideration 2

The text itself is important to fostering a critical literacy stance, by making possible certain intellectual and social work (Muhammad, 2020). For emergent bilingual youth, the images in the graphic novels supported them to interrogate objective violence and analyze how meanings and worldviews get produced. The visual content made it easier for emergent bilingual youth to approach graphic novels as artistic *representations* of the social world – created by a person or persons with social identities and agendas.

Consideration 3

The jury trial encouraged youth to explore multiple perspectives – their own perspectives, the perspectives of the characters in the graphic novel, and the perspectives of the graphic novelist. It is important to emphasize, as Lori did, that the jury trial is not meant to produce a "winner or loser." That is, the goal of critical literacy pedagogy is not to arrive at a single, definitive solution, but to grapple with many, oftentimes competing and contradictory discourses – in this case, discourses surrounding gender and sexual violence. Some of these discourses may be dominant/hegemonic, but others are counter-hegemonic.

Consideration 4

In addition to the jury trial, the graphic novel unit was mostly made up of whole-class discussions and small-group explorations, in which students grappled with not only their own, but the graphic novel's discourses surrounding gender, sexual violence, and power. Lori asked questions such as, "Why is Alan Moore putting stuff like this [scenes of rape]?" She invited students to write about Alan Moore's views on women and their stance on Alan Moore's views. Lori's questions were not fact-based nor meant to evaluate students' comprehension of content– for example, asking students to name the main characters. While Lori did ensure that students understood the content and context, she posed questions that prompted students to explore how they felt and what they thought about the representations in the text. This means that teachers have to move away from what Paulo Freire famously called the banking model.

Consideration 5

There were instances when youth voiced discourses that were alarming and triggering – surfacing dominant ideologies that blamed women for their profession, behavior, and/or dress, or that positioned women as either passive recipients or assertive gatekeepers. Because of the unpredictability and dangers, teachers are often nervous about surfacing issues of consent, desire, and sexual violence (Clonan-Roy et al., 2021), choosing instead to teach from a textbook. Instead of attempting to remove risk, which is impossible in critical literacy pedagogy, we have to accept that critical literacy pedagogy will surface emotions – students' and teacher's – such as fear, discomfort, defensiveness, embarrassment, and even pleasure. This is because critical literacy pedagogy asks students and the teacher to confront texts and ideas that may go against the very "fiber of their beliefs" (Janks, 2002, p. 19).

Rather than dismiss feelings as secondary to logic or as an obstacle to learning, Lori often asked students to write in their journal – How is this scene in the graphic novel making you feel? How is this discussion making you feel? Where is that feeling coming from? Furthermore, teachers have to communicate, often and explicitly, that these discussions are not about "fixing" students and their beliefs. Instead, Lori shared stories about the mindset she grew up with and what made her question or change them. She also reminded youth that everyone is still learning and developing – akin to the idea that "contradictory modes of thinking characterize the way most people view the world" (Giroux, 2003, p. 55).

To create a courageous classroom space, Lori invited students to co-develop the classroom norms and rules for engaging in "daring conversations" (Ashcraft, 2012). This practice was for all of her classes and units. While every class develops its own norms and community agreements, the most common ones include norms like, "No name calling," "Treating everyone with respect," "Listening," "Apologize if you hurt someone's feelings" and "Don't interrupt. It's rude!" And while we believe that it is impossible to remove all risk in critical literacy classrooms, in hindsight, we would have put more care into supporting students emotionally– for example, issuing trigger and content warnings and building community agreements that pay attention to students' emotional safety (e.g., sitting out a discussion).

Conclusion

In this chapter, I've made both prescriptive and descriptive claims, arguing for a critical literacy and multimodal pedagogy and a focus on objective violence, as well as describing, with empirical examples, youth as they grappled with the various discourses that normalize sexual violence. I also offered a set of practices and considerations in critical literacy pedagogy, including the central role of texts, and the use of whole-class discussions and projects that go beyond "right/wrong" or "winner/loser." But in closing, I bring the gaze inward—to myself and Lori. In order to design spaces where youth can interrogate objective violence in the world, we ourselves had to constantly engage in critical literacy practices—critically (re)reading our own autobiographies and processes of socialization around sex and sexual violence. We had to go beyond personal reflection, and instead embrace critical reflexivity—probing the "links between forms of education and the perpetuation of rape culture" (Clonan-Roy et al., 2021, p. 244) and our own role in upholding or dismantling that link.

References

Alim, H. S. (2010). Critical language awareness. In N. Hornberger & S. L. McKay (Eds.,) *Sociolinguistics and language education* (pp. 205-231). Multilingual Matters.

Anwaruddin, S. M. (2016). Interrupting the conditions of sexual violence: Towards a critical literacy approach to pedagogy. *Society and Culture in South Asia, 2*(2), 256-275.

Ashcraft, C. (2012). But how do we talk about it?: Critical literacy practices for addressing sexuality with youth. *Curriculum Inquiry, 42*(5), 597-628.

Ayers, W. (2019). I shall create! Teaching toward freedom. In L. Delpit (Ed.,) *Teaching when the world is on fire* (pp. 3-15). The New Press.

Baker-Bell, A. (2020). *Linguistic justice: Black language, literacy, identity, and pedagogy*. Routledge.

Behrman, E. H. (2006). Teaching about language, power, and text: A review of classroom practices that support critical literacy. *Journal of Adolescent & Adult literacy, 49*(6), 490-498.

Clonan-Roy, K., Goncy, E. A., Naser, S. C., Fuller, K. A., DeBoard, A., Williams, A., & Hall, A. (2021). Preserving abstinence and preventing rape: How sex education textbooks contribute to rape culture. *Archives of sexual behavior, 50*, 231-245.

Cochran-Smith, M., & Lytle, S. L. (2009). *Inquiry as stance: Practitioner research for the next generation*. Teachers College Press.

Colantonio-Yurko, K., Boehm, S. & Olmstead, K. (2022) Girls rising: Addressing female activist characters in YA literature through critical literacy, *The Clearing House: A Journal of Educational Strategies, Issues and Ideas, 95*(3), 136-141.

Flores, N., & Rosa, J. (2015). Undoing appropriateness: Raciolinguistic ideologies and language diversity in education. *Harvard Educational Review, 85*(2), 149-171.

García, O., Johnson, S. I., & Seltzer, K. (2017). *The translanguaging classroom: Leveraging student bilingualism for learning.* Caslon.

García, O., & Kleifgen, J. A. (2018). *Educating emergent bilinguals: Policies, programs, and practices for English learners.* Teachers College Press.

Gee, J. P. (2004). Learning language as a matter of learning social languages within discourses. *Language learning and teacher education: A sociocultural approach*, 13-31.

Giroux, H. (2003). Critical theory and education practice. In A. Darder, M. Baltodano, & R. D. Torres (Eds.), *The critical pedagogy reader* (pp. 27–56). Routledge.

Janks, H. (2002). Critical literacy: Beyond reason. *The Australian Educational Researcher,* 29(1), 7–26.

Janks, H., Dixon, K., Ferreira, A., Granville, S., & Newfield, D. (2013). *Doing critical literacy: Texts and activities for students and teachers.* Routledge.

Low, D. E., Lyngfelt, A., Thomas, A., & Vasquez, V. M. (2021). Critical Literacy and Contemporary Literatures. In J.Z. Pandya, R. A. Mora, J.H. Alford, N.A. Golden, & R. S. De Roock (Eds.). (2021). *The handbook of critical literacies* (pp. 308-316). Routledge.

Luke, A. (2004). Two takes on the critical. In B. Norton & K. Toohey (Eds.), *Critical pedagogies and language learning* (pp. 21–29). Cambridge University Press

Luke, A. (2018). *Critical literacy, schooling, and social justice: The selected works of Allan Luke.* Routledge.

Makoni, B. (2011). Multilingual miniskirt discourses in motion: the discursive construction of the female body in public space. *International Journal of Applied Linguistics,* 21(3), 340-359.

Meier, G. S. (2017). The multilingual turn as a critical movement in education: Assumptions, challenges and a need for reflection. *Applied Linguistics Review,* 8(1), 131–161.

Manduley, A. E., Mertens, A., Plante, I., & Sultana, A. (2018). The role of social media in sex education: Dispatches from queer, trans, and racialized communities. *Feminism & Psychology,* 28(1), 152-170.

Muhammad, G. (2020). *Cultivating genius: An equity framework for culturally and historically responsive literacy.* Scholastic Incorporated.

Paris, D., & Alim, H. S. (Eds.). (2017). *Culturally sustaining pedagogies: Teaching and learning for justice in a changing world.* Teachers College Press.

Park, J. Y. (2016). "Breaking the word" and "sticking with the picture": Critical literacy education of US immigrant youth with graphic novels. *English Teaching: Practice & Critique,* 15(1), 91-104.

Park, J. Y. (2023). *Educating Emergent Bilingual Youth in High School: The Promise of Critical Language and Literacy Education.* Routledge.

Phipps, A., Ringrose, J., Renold, E., & Jackson, C. (2018). Rape culture, lad culture and everyday sexism: Researching, conceptualizing and politicizing new mediations of gender and sexual violence. *Journal of Gender Studies, 27*(1), 1-8.

Ralfe, E. (2009). Policy: Powerful or pointless? An exploration of the role of critical literacy in challenging and changing gender stereotypes. *Language Learning Journal, 37*(3), 305-321.

Suárez-Orozco, C., Suárez-Orozco, M. M., & Todorova, I. (2008). *Learning a new land: Immigrant students in American society.* Harvard University Press.

Young, J. P. (2000). Boy talk: Critical literacy and masculinities. *Reading Research Quarterly, 35*(3), 312-337.

Young, J. P. (2001). Displaying practices of masculinity: Critical literacy and social contexts. *Journal of Adolescent & Adult Literacy, 45*(1), 4-14.

Žižek, S. (2008). *Violence: Six sideways reflections.* Profile Books

Žižek, S. (2016). Language, violence and nonviolence. *International Journal of Žižek Studies, 2*(3), 1-12.

"It shouldn't take you personally knowing a potential victim to start being a decent person": Exploring the Importance of Vulnerability in Critical Literacy Learning

Brittany Adams, The University of Alabama

Introduction

When Nadia (a pseudonym) joined a freshman book study that I facilitated in the fall of 2019, it was in pursuit of knowledge. The book study centered a young adult novel focused on systemic sexual violence and rape culture, a concept that Nadia was working to understand. Throughout the experience, she approached discussions with an analytical perspective and was socially invested in the group's collective understanding.. Throughout the book study, she insisted that her own life had been untouched by rape culture, and she almost never explicitly drew on personal or cultural resources to make sense of the text, group discussion, or her own understanding. Her initial positioning and understanding of the major topics never seemed to evolve throughout the semester. However, I struggled to understand Nadia's experience because she rarely showed me her sense-making. Interestingly, Nadia was the participant who proposed an action project that the entire group ended up working on, making her participation and experience all the more confounding to me.

In this chapter, I strive to untangle my perceptions of Nadia and our diverging perspectives on what makes for a successful learning experience—namely, vulnerability of self. It is my hope that reflecting on and troubling my own assumptions about Nadia will function as a reminder to other critical pedagogues that there are both limitations to this work as well as infinite ways that learning might manifest. Her experience in the book study invites important questions about what critical literacy looks like and what it means to be critical.

Critical Literacy and Young Adult Literature

To further understand the foundations of these diverging perspectives (mine and Nadia's) and the role of vulnerability in learning, it is essential to explore the concept of critical literacy as framed by key theorists in the field. A key outcome of Freire's (1970) critical pedagogy, critical literacy refers to the ability to actively analyze texts to better understand power, inequality, and injustice in human relationships, with the explicit aim of "transformation of dominant ideologies, cultures and economies, and institutions and political systems" (Luke, 2012, p. 5). In defining literacy as "reading the word and the world", Freire and Macedo (1987) recognized that literacy is more than learning to read and write: that it includes understanding what one reads and connecting said understanding to the world for the purpose of empowerment. Such instruction can be agentive and emancipatory through enabling students to interpret the complex social powers at play in texts, think critically, and take action to change unjust situations.

Since the 1970s, Freire's work has been taken up by many critical pedagogues and critical literacy scholars to advocate for teaching students how to consider the social, political, and economic powers at play (Luke, 2012). Sociocultural definitions of literacy argue that literacy is always about ways of participating in social and cultural groups (Gee, 2017). Language, in all its forms and modalities, indexes humanity within social relationships (Bakhtin, 1981, 1986; Vygotsky, 1978). Students bring culturally constructed knowledge and values into the classroom (Heath, 2011; Moll et al., 2009; Street, 1985). Thus, participation in literacy instruction both shapes and is shaped by the student. Several critical literacy educators have developed curricula to guide students in critiquing and revising dominant discourses (e.g., Janks, et al., 2013; Lewison et al., 2015; McLaughlin & DeVoogd, 2004; Vasquez et al., 2013). These scholars demonstrate exciting possibilities for critical literacy instruction, even though effectively teaching critical literacy in the classroom has continued to present a challenge to teachers because critical literacies operate from sociocultural definitions of literacy while learning objectives tend to focus on decontextualized skills and strategies (Avila & Moore, 2012).

There remains a surprising dearth of research on implementing these critical literacy instructional models in higher education contexts. Yet, one would think that higher education is an essential space for critical literacy education, as it may well be the last institutional space in which entrenched ways of thinking about the world might be challenged (Wallin-Rushchman, 2014). I opted to draw on Lewison and colleagues' (2015) model of critical literacy pedagogy to guide the curriculum developed in this study. They conceptualize critical literacy as a transaction between three components: the personal and cultural resources readers bring to and draw on while reading (e.g., personal experiences, prior knowledge); the critical practices readers enact while reading (disrupting commonplace thinking, interrogating multiple viewpoints, focusing on the sociopolitical, and envisioning action for social justice); and the critical stance that readers are able to demonstrate while reading and when out in the world (e.g., reflexivity, inquiry, considering alternative perspectives).

Although the body of serious literary criticism focused on young adult literature (YAL) is ever-expanding, it is still infrequently offered "the respect of the scholarship and acceptance that is given to classic and emerging literature written specifically for adults" in higher education settings (Bickmore, 2014, p. x). However, there is a growing recognition of YAL's value as an entry point into critical literacies for college students because of its ability to demystify complex social issues (Adams, 2020; Chisholm & Cook, 2021; Fletcher, 2021; Zdilla, 2010). The events and character experiences described in young adult literature (YAL) function as "vicarious experiences" (Gee, 2017, p. 38) where readers can find their perspectives on the world expanded. This is particularly important for trauma narratives, as reading a novel about police brutality or sex trafficking significantly lowers the "cost of failure," (Gee, 2017, p. 71) so students can explore, take mental and emotional risks, and empathize with others without experiencing trauma first-hand.

Many educators leverage YAL to teach about critical social issues or taboo topics, such as death (e.g., Beckelhimer, 2017), immigration and deportation (e.g., Rodríguez, 2019), eating disorders (e.g., Collins & Lazard, 2020), religious discrimination (e.g., Ginsberg & Glenn, 2019), and still other disturbing topics (Ivey & Johnston, 2018). More pertinent to this study, numerous scholars have taken up YAL as a pedagogical avenue for discussing sexual harassment and assault with students who are often socialized into harmful beliefs about victims and survivors (e.g., Adams, 2020; Alsup, 2003; Cleveland & Durand, 2014; Colantonio-Yurko, et al. 2018; Jackett, 2007; Malo-Juvera, 2014; Park, 2012). Such studies demonstrate how adolescents and young adults can alter their thinking and disrupt dangerous misconceptions about sexual violence.

Vulnerability

Vulnerability has emerged as a significant concept within the realm of teaching and learning, influencing pedagogical practices and educational research. Defined as the willingness to expose oneself to uncertainty, risk, and emotional discomfort, vulnerability plays a crucial role in fostering authentic engagement, meaningful connections, and transformative learning experiences (Brown, 2012). Within educational contexts, vulnerability is not merely an individual trait but also a relational and contextual phenomenon that shapes the dynamics of classrooms and learning environments. In recent years, scholars and educators have increasingly recognized the importance of creating spaces where students feel safe to embrace vulnerability and share their authentic selves (Johnson, 2014). Drawing on the principles of relational pedagogy, educators emphasize the significance of building trusting relationships and nurturing a sense of belonging within the classroom community (Biesta, 2013). By acknowledging and honoring students' lived experiences, identities, and perspectives, educators can create inclusive learning environments that validate diverse voices and foster empathetic understanding (hooks, 1994).

Moreover, vulnerability intersects with notions of power, privilege, and social justice within educational settings. Critical pedagogues argue that vulnerability is inherently linked to processes of social transformation and liberation (Freire, 1970). By encouraging students to critically examine their own positions within systems of oppression and privilege, educators can empower them to challenge dominant narratives, interrogate structural inequities, and advocate for social change (Giroux, 2011). However, fostering vulnerability in the pursuit of critical consciousness requires a nuanced understanding of the complex intersections of identity, power, and resistance (Gutiérrez, 2008).

Furthermore, research indicates that vulnerability is not equally experienced by all students within educational contexts. Marginalized individuals, including those from racial, ethnic, socioeconomic, or LGBTQ+ communities, may navigate heightened levels of vulnerability due to systemic inequalities and social injustices (Valenzuela, 1999). Conversely, students who occupy positions of privilege may face challenges in recognizing and confronting their own complicity in perpetuating oppression (DiAngelo, 2018). Therefore, educators must attend to the differential vulnerabilities experienced by students based on their intersecting social identities and positionalities.

In practice, fostering vulnerability in teaching and learning requires intentional pedagogical strategies and supportive classroom environments. Cultivating a culture of trust, empathy, and reciprocity is foundational to creating spaces where students feel empowered to take intellectual risks, engage in difficult dialogues, and embrace vulnerability as a catalyst for growth (DeMeulenaere, 2023). Additionally, educators can leverage experiential learning, reflective practices, and collaborative inquiry to scaffold students' journeys toward vulnerability and self-discovery (Jagers et al., 2021).

In sum, the literature on critical literacy, young adult literature, and vulnerability provides a robust framework for understanding and fostering transformative learning experiences. In reflecting on Nadia's experience in the freshman book study, several critical insights emerge about the multifaceted nature of learning, vulnerability, and critical literacy. As a result, this case underscores the importance of recognizing diverse manifestations of learning and critical consciousness.

Methods

Teaching and Research Context

This study took place at a major southern institution during a semester-long optional book study for undergraduates. My intentions for the group of freshmen who joined the book study were twofold. First, I wanted to offer new college students a space to learn about and discuss rape culture, a high-profile topic following the explosion of sexual assault allegations in 2017 against powerful figures (Carlsen et al., 2018; Rummler, 2020). Second, I sought to better understand the impact of critical literacy pedagogy designed around young adult literature. Taking advantage of a university program, I designed a one-credit, discussion-based 'course' around a single book (essentially, a book club). Such courses were not required and were graded as pass/fail, so those who signed up did so by choice. They were popular with freshmen and sophomore students who were adjusting to college life and taking general education courses.

Throughout the semester, students read, wrote about, and discussed Amy Reed's YA novel *The Nowhere Girls* (2017). Through the story of Lucy, a girl run out of town for accusing a group of popular high school boys of gang rape, the novel disrupts commonplace thinking by positing that sexual violence is frequent and the result of cultural norms that celebrate dominance. It interrogates multiple viewpoints by providing a multiplicity of character voices who have varying and often conflicting perspectives and opinions about sexual assault, particularly regarding how it connects to social norms related to gender and sexuality. When the protagonists are repeatedly rebuffed in their attempts to seek justice for Lucy and other victims, it focuses on the sociopolitical by illuminating how social and political factors influence people's decisions and lives and how unequal power relationships reify rape culture. Finally, the protagonists' experiences trying to change the culture at the school by going on strike demonstrate multiple examples of taking action to disrupt inequitable conditions.

Every Thursday, I met with 15 students from a wide variety of majors to discuss the novel, tell stories, and share perspectives. Discussions were scheduled to last an hour but sometimes ran a few minutes longer. Much of our weekly meeting time was dedicated to small- and whole-group discussion. McLaughlin and DeVoogd (2004) provide some generic questions which teachers can use to engage in critical analysis, such as "Whose voices are represented? Whose voices are marginalized or discounted?" and "How can the reader use this information to promote equity?" (p. 41). While these questions were helpful starting points, students were invited to propose their own discussion questions to allow their interests to drive discussion. Though I could not predict or control what personal or cultural resources students would bring with them, I encouraged them to draw on their personal experiences, prior knowledge, and pop culture and media interests. I also consistently encouraged students to consider what actions might be taken in response to what they were learning. Nadia, the focal student of this chapter, was one of these 15 students.

Research Design and Data Collection

The larger study that yielded the data explored in this chapter was a qualitative multi-case case study (Stake, 2005) of individuals in the book study. Data collected included field notes from weekly group meetings, participant journals kept throughout the book study, and transcripts from one approximately 60-minute semi-structured interview with each participant after the book study concluded. Interviews took place at the end of the semester and focused on participants' experiences during the book study and their perspectives at its conclusion. Audio recordings were not feasible during book study meetings because the large number of participants created significant crosstalk that made transcription and participant identification a challenge. I was the primary instrument of data collection, recording field notes in real time and conducting the one-on-one interviews.

Data Analysis

First round coding of each data source generated a list of open codes rooted directly in the data (Stake, 2005). Then, I engaged in several rounds of review of the code list, guided by the components of Lewison and colleagues' (2015) model of critical literacy. As data analysis concluded, codes were collapsed and sorted into themes related to the major categories from Lewison and colleagues' (2015) framework, as well as one additional category that focused on the specific context of the study. As this article examines a subset of data from the multi-case study, I explore only the themes pertinent to Nadia (see Adams, 2020; 2021; 2024 for additional information).

Positionality Statement

In qualitative research, the researcher's experiences and personal theoretical frame- works inevitably impact interpretation. This work in undoubtedly informed by my belief that rape culture is a real phenomenon. I believe that rape is pervasive and normalized due to societal attitudes about gender and sexuality. It has been documented for decades (Buchwald et al., 2005; Smith, 2004) and has material impacts on people's lives. I believe there is a culture of silence (Freire, 1970) around discussions of sexual assault that prevents victims from learning the language of critique necessary to challenge rape culture, perpetuating oppression. As a result, the common conception of rape remains binary and episodic. My commitment to this issue is both personal and political. Research is never neutral, and I believe I have an ethical obligation to challenge inequitable systems.

Findings

Data analysis for the larger study on which this paper reflects showed that all participants demonstrated some features of critical literacy as identified by Lewison and colleagues (2015). To varying degrees of success, participants drew from personal resources, developed a critical stance, and demonstrated critical social practices (Adams, 2020; 2021). While some participants demonstrated their progress through external acts, such as challenging power structures and instigating dialogue, other participants' growth was more internal in terms of their understanding of themselves, their relation to others, and their relation to the social and political environment. Furthermore, every participant expressed desire to move beyond merely understanding rape culture to disrupting it.

What each student got from the experience appeared to be related to the personal and cultural resources they brought to the experience, their previous understandings of systems of power in society, and their roles or positions within those systems. While participant journeys differed from person to person, the following sections will illuminate how Nadia's trajectory stood in stark contrast to others in the group. Yet, partway through the semester, Nadia proposed, and the class agreed, that the entire class would work on an action project together. In this section I examine the personal and cultural resources Nadia brought to the experience, followed by the critical stance she developed and the critical social practices she engaged in.

Personal and Cultural Resources

Nadia self-identified as an Indian American cishet woman majoring in computer science, Nadia signed up for the book study because "the novel looked interesting and like it would lead to meaningful discussions." She wrote, "I am fortunate to say that rape culture hasn't affected me as I have lived in a small, protected community for most of my life, but people need to know about these things. It is important to me to be well-versed in topics important in society." Her position throughout the book study remained that of someone who was fortunate have no experience with rape culture but who still wanted to be well informed and articulate about the issue.

Nadia was looking for the book study to provide "rich discussions and relatable anecdotes" that would strengthen her "ability to engage in discussions about rape culture that will undoubtedly come up in the future." This was a typical place to start. However, the first several weeks revealed Nadia's singular focus on the assigned readings as the basis for her journals and discussion contributions. Despite encouraging her to use the text to connect to the world around her, she remained more in line with formalist New Criticism (e.g., Wellek & Warren, 1949) than the reader-response theory (Rosenblatt, 2004) that contributed to the foundations of critical literacy. In this, she showed a talent for analyzing the novel, both its content and form. She asked questions like, "I wonder about the choice of the author to remain in third person for all characters, when the standard in young adult literature is first person? Are these conscious decisions that are intended to evoke certain connotations?" While her questions revealed her skills at critical thinking and analysis, they told me very little about her sensemaking of major concepts covered in the book.

During a class conversation about good and bad parenting, Nadia brought up the television show *Friends*, saying, "All six of the main characters had and raised children in unconventional ways. I think parenting is relative." This was a rare occasion when I was able to consider what the resources she drew from meant about her sense-making. Unfortunately, they were so few and far between that I really struggled to gain even a basic profile of Nadia. As she continued to contribute to discussions and appear socially invested in the major concepts, I grew concerned that I was missing something. Was she just a private person? As a White educator working with Nadia, I wondered was it a matter of cultural difference? She didn't appear resistant to thoughts and opinions that were expressed in the readings and in class discussions, but she also showed very little of her own feelings on the book study topics. While most participants came to discussions bursting with revelations and connections to their own life, Nadia appeared much more comfortable exploring the feelings and experiences of others. Was I perhaps inadvertently imposing my cultural norms and expectations on this student from a different background, and thereby misinterpreting their engagement (Frankenberg, 1993; Leonardo, 2002)?

Her interview after the book study ended was the shortest of all the interviews I conducted. She responded to my protocol while still revealing very little about herself. When asked about her family, she told me what her parents did for a living. When asked about her hobbies, she talked about her career plans in computer science. She repeated how important the book study was because "people need to know about these things." In her journals, discussion, and interview she often used general language like "people" and "society" rather than terms that made the book study and its major topics more of a personal experience.

Perhaps the most revealing thing she said to me came at the end of her interview. I mentioned that she wrote significantly more about the texts and less about herself than many of the other students and asked why she thought that might be. She grimaced and said,

> "In an essay about Virginia Woolf, Rebecca Solnit talks about how it's braver to admit that you aren't sure rather than pretend to know something you don't. It made me think about how growing up when my parents or teachers or friends would ask me a question, whether it was on something I had read, or something I was supposed to do,

or something I should have known...if I didn't know the answer, I would try to just make something up really quick [laughs] and I think I still have that same paranoia about getting caught not knowing something that I should know."

This comment potentially sheds some light on how Nadia experienced the book study. I suspect that Nadia was insecure about her prior knowledge coming into the experience and intimidated by the complexity of the major concepts. She seemed to agree in theory with the idea that there is strength in vulnerability, but I perceived how challenging it was in practice to make herself vulnerable to the book study group.

Critical Social Practices and Critical Stance

Compared to other members of the book study group, Nadia's data rarely yielded clear evidence of critical stance (e.g., recognizing one's unconscious frames, considering one's role in maintaining the status quo) or engaged in critical social practices (e.g., asking what systems of meaning are operating, reflecting on multiple and contradictory perspectives). During coding, I made a point to question my own coding process and consult with colleagues about what I was seeing in her data. I believe that her choice of enrolling in the book study to strengthen her "ability to engage in discussions about rape culture" represents a nascent critical stance and first steps toward critical social practices. I believe this is true for all students who participated in the book study. To some degree, Nadia recognized the need to problematize commonplace thinking about sexual assault and gendered violence and made the conscious decision to sign up for a book study about the topic. By enrolling, she seemed to be asking what discourses and systems of meaning are taking place in society about sexual assault.

Additionally, she often contributed to classroom conversations that revolved around thinking about sexual assault in sociopolitical terms. However, I struggled to code those discussion contributions as evidence of her recognition that politics, sociopolitical systems, power, and language are entangled in our understanding of sexual assault or considering how privilege, power, and injustice impact ideas about sexual assault commonly held in society. Her contributions, while not insubstantial, were benign. For example, in a small group discussion about how men often only begin to care about sexual harassment and assault when they realize it could happen to their sister or daughter, Nadia commented, "It shouldn't take you personally knowing a potential victim to start being a decent person." In many ways, that statement seemed to be Nadia's major motivation for participating in the book study. She described being personally unaffected by rape culture but believed that people should be aware of it.

No matter how broadly I coded, her contributions never seemed to add up to conclusive evidence of critical stance. At times, I wondered if she already grasped the complex social and political systems that interacted to foster a culture of rape and was operating several steps ahead of her peers. At others, I wondered if she was wanting to present as someone who understood the issues around rape culture without having to do the work necessary to internalize it. Yet, while other participants revealed their sensemaking and the internal struggle of integrating new ideas into preexisting worldviews, Nadia did not provide evidence of that nature. In fact, some of her comments made me suspect she wasn't putting much effort into making sense of major concepts. One day in small groups, all of Nadia's group members felt that a certain character perspective in the novel seemed more emotional and biased (i.e., it relied less on facts and logical argumentation) than others they had read up to that point. Nadia responded, "I didn't notice it when I was reading, but now that you bring it up, I can see it." This response could be interpreted as Nadia being open to entertaining alternative perspectives presented by her peers. Alternatively, it could represent her disinterest in doing the cognitive labor necessary to make sense of all the concurrent perspectives present in discourse about sexual assault and rape culture.

In a discussion about Dr. Christine Blasey Ford's allegations of sexual assault committed by Supreme Court nominee, Brett Kavanaugh, Nadia told her small group, "I didn't watch the trial live, but I read articles summarizing it. I want to go back and watch some of the footage myself now, especially after hearing all your different takes." Did this represent Nadia's slow progress toward taking responsibility to inquire? Or was this merely performance for her peers? Nadia seemed to embrace the beliefs that undergirded the book study—at least, she never expressly challenged them—but her superficial understanding of the material circumstances of rape culture belied her investment. In one journal entry she wrote, "I think women are just starting to take a stand on this issue and we are finally making our voices heard. The term 'feminist' is now in everyone's lexicon." This statement seemed to disregard centuries of women's rights activism and sexual assault advocacy, undeterred by the novel explicitly situating current discourse about rape culture within historical contexts.

Yet, despite what appeared to be shallow engagement in the major concepts, Nadia consistently asked action-oriented questions geared toward disrupting rape culture. At various points, she wondered, "Is it possible for the girls [in the YA novel] to change the view of the entire school?", "What will it take to stop victim blaming?", and "Is this recent attention and discussion about rape culture actually changing anything or is it all just talk?" She often thought about the issues under discussion in terms of action. In a journal entry following the group discussion about Brett Kavanaugh's congressional hearing, she wrote, "A positive outcome [of the hearing and surrounding media attention] is the overwhelming encouragement from young people to urge their friends to register and vote." Though she never explicitly commented on her own complicity in maintaining rape culture, the reminder she identified for herself was to "Call people out if they say inappropriate things, even if it's in the form of jokes." I was left with the impression that Nadia wanted to bypass the work of understanding the intimacies and complexities of rape culture in order to skip right to taking action.

In fact, in the most surprising turn of the events, Nadia was the one who proposed creating an informational video about consent that the entire class participated in making. Halfway through the semester, I placed her in a small group with some other students who had started asking questions about what we, as individuals, could do to challenge rape culture. I suggested that their small group start a list of things we, as individuals or as a whole, could reasonably do to engender change. I was imagining them coming up with small reminders for the group, such as asking friends to call when they got home safely. Instead, they discussed how we don't have the power to change sexual education policies in K-12 schooling but that we could encourage frank talks about sex and assault on the university campus. Throughout the book study, there had been several references to a video that the university shows at every freshman orientation. The video, entitled "Consent: It's Simple as Tea", is a publicly available 2-minute clip that uses an analogy to equate consent with serving a guest tea (May, 2015). For example, one line from the video says, "If they say 'no, thank you' then don't make them tea." Throughout the semester the class had come to agree that the video, while shown at orientation with good intentions, left something to be desired when it came to fostering open dialogue and a culture of consent on campus.

When the small groups came together for a whole class discussion, Nadia addressed the entire group for the first time all semester,

> "Our group discussed how the issue with short-term solutions to rape culture is that they are just quick fixes when what we really need are ideas that can disrupt rape culture, not just reduce rapes. Something we thought we could do as a class to change the culture on campus was to write a letter to the orientation committee about why the tea video isn't enough and how they could do better."

I responded positively to this idea but pushed them to think it through, saying, "That sounds like a great idea. What would you suggest they do instead of the tea video?" Everyone was silent for a moment while they thought. Then Nadia tentatively suggested, "What if we made our own video to offer them to replace the tea video?" This was met with resounding agreement and excitement from the class at large. After some negotiating and giving students time to think about the enormity of the undertaking, I agreed to let the entire class work on the video project in the final weeks of the semester.

From then on, Nadia was very engaged in the video making process. She sent me several emails with resources and ideas. She was also very outspoken in brainstorming sessions about collecting and selecting information to include in the video and script writing. This observable shift from shallow engagement during discussion to deep engagement in the action project is what makes Nadia's experience singular. In terms of critical literacy, what does it mean if a person is taking action to disrupt and transform inequities, but they aren't demonstrating critical stance or engaged in the other three critical social practices? I was compelled to ask myself, as both an educator and researcher, if I am making space for my students and participants to be critical in different ways? Was I dismissing Nadia's version of criticality because it didn't fit my framework?

I returned to the literature that informed this study to seek clarity. Freire (2014) believes that critical consciousness begins with growing awareness of systemic inequities. At the core of this awakening is reflection, which he defines as the continuous negotiation of the self in relation to the world. Reflection is the process by which individuals deconstruct the social and political environment and their position in and relationship to the environment. According to Freire (2014), reflection must precede taking action against oppressive elements. Otherwise, those actions aren't informed by the understanding of the self and the relation of the self to society. Lewison, Flint and Van Sluys (2002) reiterate that one cannot take informed action against oppression or promote social justice without expanded understandings and perspectives gained from the other three critical social practices.

However, Johnson and Vasudevan (2012) argue that "critical literacy is an embodied performance that is always and already occurring, regardless of whether or not it is recognized as such" (p. 36). While her data provided little evidence of her reflection process, making it challenging for me to recognize the extent by which her action was informed by her understanding of herself and her relation to the social and political environment, her engagement in the action project represents some degree of embodied critical literacy. Her contribution to the class was undeniably meaningful. Perhaps Nadia was more comfortable engaging in the project because it took the onus off her being able to articulate understanding and explore her personal history. Perhaps her insecurity about not having the right answers hindered her ability to use the journals and class discussions in the way I designed. If the journal entries had been private, would her written work have been the same? It requires reconsideration of my curriculum and praxis to ensure that I am making space for all my students' lived and embodied critical literacy practices (Johnson & Vasudevan, 2012).

Nadia, unsurprisingly, was satisfied with the action project, saying, "I felt like all semester I was asking, what can we do? So, having that action project at the end was a comfort to know that there are things we can do and are doing." If not for Nadia's relentless pushing toward action, the conclusion of the book study would have been an entirely different, and I suspect less powerful, experience.

Discussion

Years later, Nadia's narrative remains a complex puzzle, prompting reflections on the multifaceted nature of identity and vulnerability in critical literacy education. I believe a degree of responsibility to inquire is necessary to even sign up for such an experience. However, beyond that, I am not confident in making assertions, positive or negative, about her critical literacy development or experience in the book study. My impression is that she wanted to focus on rape culture as a social issue but did not want to think about herself as a participant in the system, something that requires often uncomfortable levels of vulnerability (Johnson, 2014). To understand that one's worldview is unique to one's experiences, one must be willing to unpack those experiences and what they mean in relation to the experiences of others. Shared vulnerability, including fear, rejection, and pain, is where opportunities for healing are born (Anwaruddin, 2016). But exposing oneself to judgment can be a frightening endeavor, especially for students who have been socialized to fear failure (Gerrity et al., 1993; Brown, 2012). While I have limited evidence that she consciously engaged, questioned commonplace thinking, practiced reflexivity, or considered alternate perspectives, that does not mean those things didn't occur. The lack of data could very well be a limitation of the study and/or instructional design.

What *is* evident is that Nadia was very interested in taking action, asking questions like "What will it take?"; "What can we do?"; "Will things ever change?" While her proposal of and participation in the class action project was notable, action that is not informed by expanded understandings gained from critical stance and the other critical social practices is not the goal of critical literacy education. Because Nadia did not show me her thinking—or perhaps I failed to see it—I struggled to understand her positioning in the book study. She reported getting a lot out of the class and enjoying it, but I am hesitant to superimpose meaning onto these assertions.

While it is enjoyable and easy to talk about what worked for participants, it is equally important to consider what did not work. It is necessary to consider the ways in which limitations of the instructor, curriculum, and context impact student success. Analysis of Nadia's course experience exposes flaws in my curriculum and my practice. The way critical literacy learning is conceptualized starts with understanding the self, and there are many reasons why students might be uncomfortable with that. Gee identifies four core aspects of identity: N identities, ones you are born with; I identities, institutionally assigned ones; D identities, ones constructed and sustained through discourse and dialogue; and A identities, ones constructed through shared experiences with affinity groups (Gee, 2001). As Hays (2018) explains, "When classroom literacy practices blur the lines between these four aspects of identity, students can experience a complicated sense of identity" (p. 54). In recognizing the complexity of identity formation within literacy practices, we can better illuminate the pathways to more inclusive and effective critical literacy learning environments.

It seems that Nadia wished to keep different aspects of her identity separate. She was willing to employ her institutional identity as a high-achieving student to achieve her desired discourse identity as someone informed of social issues like rape culture. However, she did not appear to want to bring her natural identities or previously established discourse identities with family and friends into the classroom. I suspect that these tensions were something Nadia grappled with, but she did not want my perception of her as a high-achieving student to be altered by her uncertainty. Nadia's trajectory reinforces the importance of critical literacy pedagogues foregrounding 'not knowing' as an essential part of literacy when in dialogue with their students. However, there may be limitations to this practice in the high-achievement grade-oriented accountability environment of higher education (Aukerman, 2012). The context of a graded classroom environment, even a pass/fail one, complicates instructor expectations of vulnerability. Literacy educators must consider these factors and the effects they have on students in order to recognize the various lived and embodied critical literacy practices they may demonstrate (Johnson & Vasudevan, 2012).

While other participant data might exemplify the potential positive outcomes of reading and discussing YAL for critical literacy education, Nadia's data illuminates the risks. Educators tend to assume that while reading diverse literature, students will notice discrepancies or contradictions between their worldview and that of characters, which will force them to "entertain alternate ways of being and take responsibility to engage in further inquiry" (Leland et al., 2018, p. 25). However, while using a novel as a springboard can be powerful, not every student will seamlessly move beyond talking about the novel as a self-contained world with no bearing on their own life.

I do believe Nadia's experience, or my experience with Nadia, speaks to the importance of student disposition as a factor in critical literacy learning. The term disposition has been variously defined as behavioral patterns (Katz, 1993); moral sensibilities (Dottin, 2006); habits of mind (Carr & Claxton, 2002); the way that beliefs shape actions in a specific context (Villegas, 2007); and "awareness, inclination and reflection on behaviors and thinking" (Schussler,

2006, p. 257). I borrow from Alsup and Miller (2014) to define dispositions as contextually and culturally specific embodied manifestations of one's beliefs, values, and judgments. It seems reasonable to assume that because this was an optional course, only people who were already pre-disposed to thinking about rape culture as a pervasive issue that implicates individuals as well as social and political systems of power would sign up. Such an assumption, if it were in fact true, might undercut the purpose of this study.

However, there is general agreement that for YAL to be a tool for critical literacy learning, students themselves must have some sort of choice in the matter (Glenn & Ginsberg, 2016; Ivey & Broaddus, 2001; Ivey & Johnston, 2013; Stover & Bach, 2011). Critical literacy cannot manifest if it is compulsory. While the participants in this study did not select the novel, they did make a choice to take the course I offered from among a variety of other course options on a wide variety of topics. Furthermore, not every participant bought in to the critical sociopolitical perspective on sexual assault. Some pushed back against course concepts as often as they agreed with them, while Nadia's sense-making was almost entirely unobservable.

One comment Nadia made in her interview gives me insight into her disposition. When asked if she had any suggestions to improve the book study experience, she said,

> "I feel like the downside of this course was that everyone was kind of on the same side. So, we didn't always talk about like common counterarguments or like loopholes in reasoning because no one was looking for them. I feel like if I were going to try to debate about this topic, I might be ready to like spit facts that I know now, but I don't know if I would be ready to entertain counterarguments because we didn't talk through them."

I believe this comment connects back to what Nadia hoped to get out of the class: "rich discussions and relatable anecdotes" that would strengthen her "ability to engage in discussions about rape culture that will undoubtedly come up in the future." It seems that her priority was being able to engage in discussions about rape culture, rather than understanding herself in relation to rape culture. While the latter will lead to the former, the reverse is not necessarily true. However, seeking a bulletproof defense of her position further strengthens my impressions of her desire for invulnerability.

Recalling Gee's (2001) four aspects of identity, Nadia wished to only take up her institutional and intellectual discourse identities in the class, not her natural identities or any other discourse identities. I suspect this is why Nadia's critical literacy development faltered, or at least was not observable to me. Engaging in the critical literacy curriculum I designed, informed by Lewison and colleagues'

(2015) framework, required investigating her own intersecting social positionings, and thus her intersecting identities. She was not predisposed to do this in front of a witness; therefore, I struggled to assess her literacy development. This begs the question: What might I have been able to offer Nadia that would have resulted in observable critical literacy development? Certainly, a pre-disposed willingness to draw from personal and cultural resources and engage in all critical social practices that the framework requires will impact student experience. However, we must also interrogate the conditions that either foster or hinder a student's display of learning because students 'perform' critical literacies (and their identities) based on how they experience relations of power and identity in the classroom context (Aukerman, 2012; Gee, 2001). For example, the university at which this research occurred is a large Predominantly White Institution, and Nadia was the only non-White presenting student in the group. This institutional and classroom also shapes the degree of vulnerability that student, especially a student of color, can safely display.

Further, Janks (2002) observed that "Where identification promises the fulfillment of desire, reason cannot compete" (p. 10). Despite the transformative aims of critical literacy, there remains a possibility that students may engage in "deconstructive reading" (p. 10) without experiencing any substantive shifts in their aspirations or behaviors. Consequently, there exists a persistent risk that discussions of power within the classroom may only scratch the surface, regardless of a teacher's intentions. Janks (2002) highlights the challenge of predicting how students will react to texts, attributing this unpredictability to the "territory beyond reason" (p. 9). This realm encompasses the intricacies of desire and identity, underscoring the important role of students' emotional relationship to social issues.

Conclusion

My experiences with Nadia challenged me to reconsider both my instruction and my orientation to this work. It is easy to fall into binary thinking when encountering unusual student behavior: either the student is participating incorrectly, or the teacher is instructing incorrectly. But just because Nadia didn't match my mental model of critical literacy doesn't mean she wasn't reading the word and the world. It does not mean she wasn't problematizing systems of power in her world. Her case prompts me to wonder: When reading in community, can critical literacy only develop through vulnerability with others in the same community? How is vulnerability to an outside audience important to developing critical literacy—can there be vulnerability without witnesses? There are innumerable reasons why someone might avoid making personal connections around rape culture, ranging from insecurity to discomfort to avoidance of uncomfortable realities. Not all students will be predisposed to make themselves vulnerable in the classroom to participate in critical literacy curriculum or otherwise. If understanding one's positionality within a social issue is necessary for critical literacy pedagogy, educators must grapple with the myriad social, cultural, and institutional functions that push students away from vulnerable reflexivity.

For educators wanting to foster vulnerability and support students in engaging with critical literacy curriculum, several concrete recommendations emerge from this experience. First, cultivating a pedagogy of trust (DeMeulenaere, 2012) is essential. This approach prioritizes the establishment of trust within the classroom environment, encouraging open dialogue, active listening, and mutual respect to create a safe space where students feel comfortable expressing themselves authentically. Second, normalizing uncertainty is crucial. Emphasizing that it's okay for students to feel uncertain or uncomfortable when engaging with complex social issues helps to create an environment where questioning and exploration are valued. Finally, validating personal experiences is key. Acknowledging and honoring the diverse experiences and perspectives of students fosters a sense of belonging and encourages students to connect their personal narratives to broader social issues.

Additionally, educators can model vulnerability by sharing their own uncertainties, mistakes, and reflections, thereby creating a culture of openness and authenticity within the classroom. Providing multiple entry points for participation allows students to engage with critical literacy curriculum in ways that resonate with them, while offering supportive feedback encourages risk-taking and growth. Promoting peer collaboration also fosters a sense of community and collective responsibility for engaging with critical issues.

While there remain many factors beyond our control or understanding, by implementing these recommendations, educators can begin developing supportive learning environment that empowers students to embrace vulnerability, critically interrogate their positionality in the world, and actively participate in critical literacy curriculum. Through trust, validation, and collaboration, we can cultivate spaces where students feel empowered to navigate complex social issues and contribute meaningfully to transformative educational experiences.

References

Adams, B. (2020). "I didn't feel confident talking about this issue…but I knew I could talk about a book": Using young adult literature to make sense of #metoo. *Journal of Literacy Research, 52*(2) 209–230.

Adams, B. (2021). Consent is not as simple as tea: Student activism against rape culture. *Girlhood Studies, 14*(1), 1-18.

Adams, B. (2024). "How am I as an individual personally processing this?": Reflective journaling for critical literacy development. *Journal of College Reading and Learning, Early View.*

Alsup, J. (2003). Politicizing young adult literature: Reading Anderson's *Speak* as a critical text. *Journal of Adolescent & Adult Literacy, 47*(2), 158-166.

Alsup, J., & Miller, S. (2014). Reclaiming English education: Rooting social justice in dispositions. *English Education, 46*(3), 195-215.

Anwaruddin, S. M. (2016). Why critical literacy should turn to 'the affective turn': Making a case for critical affective literacy. *Discourse: Studies in the Cultural Politics of Education, 37*(3), 381–396.

Aukerman, M. (2012). "Why do you say yes to Pedro, but no to me?" Toward a critical literacy of dialogic engagement. *Theory Into Practice, 51*(1), 42-48.

Avila, J., & Moore, M. (2012). Critical literacy, digital literacies, and common core state standards: A workable union?. *Theory Into Practice, 51*(1), 27-33.

Bakhtin, M. M. (1981). *The dialogic imagination: Four essays* (M. Holquist, Ed.; C. Emerson & M. Holquist, Trans). The University of Texas Press.

Bakhtin, M. M. (1986). *Speech genres and other late essays.* (V. W. McGee, Trans). The University of Texas Press.

Beckelhimer, L. (2017). One teacher's experiences: responding to death through language. *English Journal, 107*(2), 41-46.

Bickmore, S. T. (2014). Foreword: Coming of age with young adult literature through critical analysis. In C. Hill (Ed.), *The critical merits of young adult literature* (pp. ix-xii). Routledge.

Biesta, G. J. J. (2013). *The beautiful risk of education.* Paradigm Publishers.

Brown, B. (2012). *Daring greatly: How the courage to be vulnerable transforms the way we live, love, parent, and lead.* Gotham Books.

Buchwald, E., Fletcher, P., & Roth, M. (Eds.). (2005). *Transforming a rape culture* (2nd ed.). Milkweed Editions.

Carlsen, A., Salam, M., Cain Miller, C., Lu, D., Ngu, A., Patel, J. K., & Wichter, Z. (2018, Oct 23). #MeToo brought down 201 powerful men. Nearly half of their replacements are women. *The New York Times.* https://www.nytimes.com/interactive/2018/10/23/us/metoo-replacements.html

Carr, M., & Claxton, G. (2002). Tracking the development of learning dispositions. *Assessment in Education, 9*(1), 9–37.

Chisholm, J. S., & Cook, M. P. (2021). Examining readers' critical literature circle discussions of *Looking for Alaska*. *Journal of Adolescent & Adult Literacy, 65*(2), 119-128.

Cleveland, E., & Durand, E. S. (2014). Critical representations of sexual assault in young adult literature. *The Looking Glass: New Perspectives on Children's Literature, 17*(3).

Colantonio-Yurko, K., Miller, C., & Cheveallier, J. (2018). "But she didn't scream": A framework for teaching about sexual assault through young adult literature. *Journal of Language and Literacy Education, 14* (1), 1-16.

Collins, M., & Lazard, A. (2020). How narrative engagement with young adult literature influences perceptions of anorexia nervosa. *Health Communication, 2020,* 1-10.

DeMeulenaere E. (2012). Toward a pedagogy of trust. In Dudley-Marling C., Michaels S. (Eds.), *High-expectation curricula: Helping all students succeed with powerful learning* (pp. 28–41). Teachers College Press.

DeMeulenaere, E. (2023). Disrupting school rituals. *Urban Education, 58*(1), 59-86.

DiAngelo, R. (2018). *White fragility: Why it's so hard for white people to talk about racism.* Beacon Press.

Dottin, E. (2006). A Deweyan approach to the development of moral dispositions in professional teacher education communities: Using a conceptual framework. In H. Sockett (Ed.), *Teacher dispositions: Building a teacher education framework for moral standards* (pp. 27–48). American Association of Colleges for Teacher Education.

Fletcher, L. (2021). "To imagine I almost said 'no'": A reluctant student's transformation using challenging texts. *Journal of Adolescent & Adult Literacy, 65*(4), 309-319.

Frankenberg, R. (1993). *White women, race matters: The social construction of whiteness.* University of Minnesota Press.

Freire, P. (1970). *Pedagogy of the oppressed* (M. Ramos, Trans.). Continuum.

Freire, P. (2014). *Education for critical consciousness.* Bloomsbury Academic.

Freire, P., & Macedo, D. (1987). *Literacy: Reading the word and the world.* Bergin & Garve.

Gee, J. (2001). Identity as an analytic lens for research in education. *Review of Research in Education, 25,* 99-125.

Gee, J. (2017). *Teaching, learning, literacy in our high-risk high-tech world: A framework for becoming human.* Teachers College Press.

Gerrity, D., Lawrence, J., & Sedlacek, W. (1993). Honors and nonhonors freshmen: Demographics, attitudes, interests, and behaviors. *NACADA Journal, 13*(1), 38–45.

Ginsberg, R., & Glenn, W. J. (2020). Moments of pause: Understanding students' shifting perceptions during a Muslim young adult literature learning experience. *Reading Research Quarterly, 55*(4), 601-623.

Giroux, H. A. (2011). *On critical pedagogy.* Bloomsbury Publishing.

Glenn, W., & Ginsberg, R. (2016). Resisting readers' identity (re)construction across English and young adult literature course contexts. *Research in the Teaching of English, 51*(1), 84-105.

Gutiérrez, K. D. (2008). Developing a sociocritical literacy in the third space. *Reading Research Quarterly, 43*(2), 148-164.

Hays, A. (2018). "Now I see them as people": Financial inequity in Eleanor & Park. *The ALAN Review, 45*(3), 53-63.

Heath, S. (2011). The book as home? It all depends. In S. Wolf, K. Coats, P. Enciso, & C. Jenkins (Eds.), *The handbook of research on children's and young adult literature* (pp. 32-47). Routledge.

hooks, b. (1994). *Teaching to transgress: Education as the practice of freedom*. Routledge.

Ivey, G., & Broaddus, K. (2001). "Just plain reading": A survey of what makes students want to read in middle school classrooms. *Reading Research Quarterly, 36*(4), 350– 377.

Ivey, G., & Johnston, P. (2013). Engagement with young adult literature: Outcomes and processes. *Reading Research Quarterly, 48*(3), 255–275.

Ivey, G., & Johnston, P. (2018). Engaging disturbing books. *Journal of Adolescent & Adult Literacy, 62*(2), 143-150.

Jackett, M. (2007). Something to speak about: Addressing sensitive issues through literature. *English Journal, 96*(4), 102-105.

Jagers, R. J., Skoog-Hoffman, A., Barthelus, B., & Schlund, J. (2021). Transformative social and emotional learning: In pursuit of educational equity and excellence. *American Educator, 45*(2), 14-19.

Janks, H. (2002). Critical literacy: Beyond reason. *The Australian Educational Researcher, 29*, 7-26.

Janks, H., Dixon, K., Ferreira, A., Granville, S., & Newfield, D. (2013). *Doing critical literacy: Texts and activities for students and teachers*. Routledge.

Johnson, E. (2014). Reconceptualizing vulnerability in personal narrative writing with youths. *Journal of Adolescent & Adult Literacy, 57*(7), 575-583.

Johnson, E., & Vasudevan, L. (2012). Seeing and hearing students' lived and embodied critical literacy practices. *Theory Into Practice, 51*(1), 34–41.

Katz, L. (1993). *Dispositions: Definitions and implications for early childhood practices*. ERIC Clearinghouse on Elementary and Early Childhood Education.

Leland, C., Lewison, M., & Harste, J. (2018). *Teaching children's literature: It's critical!* (2nd ed.). Routledge.

Leonardo, Z. (2002). The souls of white folk: Critical pedagogy, whiteness studies, and globalization discourse. *Race Ethnicity and Education, 5*(1), 29-50.

Lewison, M., Flint, A., & Van Sluys, K. (2002). Taking on critical literacy: The journey of newcomers and novices. *Language Arts, 79*(5), 382–392.

Lewison, M., Leland, C., & Harste, J. (2015). *Creating critical classrooms: Reading and writing with an edge* (2nd ed.). Routledge.

Luke, A. (2012). Critical literacy: Foundational notes. *Theory into Practice, 51*(1), 4-11.
Malo-Juvera, V. (2014). *Speak*: The effect of literacy instruction on adolescents' rape myth acceptance. *Research in the Teaching of English, 48*(4), 407-27.
May, E. [Blue Seat Studios]. (2015, May 12). Consent: It's simple as tea [Video file]. Retrieved from https://www.youtube.com/watch?v=oQbei5JGiT8
McLaughlin, M., & DeVoogd, G. (2004). *Critical literacy: Enhancing students' comprehension of text*. Scholastic.
Moll, L., Amanti, C., Neff, D., & Gonzalez, N. (2009). Funds of knowledge for teaching: Using a qualitative approach to connect homes and classrooms. *Theory Into Practice, 31*, 132-141.
Park, J. Y. (2012). Re-imaging reader-response in middle and secondary schools: Early adolescent girls' critical and communal reader responses to the young adult novel *Speak*. *Children's Literature in Education, 43*(3), 191- 212.
Reed, A. (2017). *The nowhere girls*. Simon & Schuster.
Rodríguez, S. A. (2019). Conocimiento narratives: Creative acts and healing in Latinx children's and young adult literature. *Children's Literature, 47*, 9-29.
Rosenblatt, L. (2004). The transactional theory of reading and writing. In R. Ruddell and N. Unrau (Eds.), *Theoretical models and processes of reading* (pp. 1363–1398). International Reading Association.
Rummler, O. (2020, Oct 27). Global #MeToo movement has resulted in 7 convictions, 5 charges of influential figures. *Axios*. https://www.axios.com/2019/09/01/global-metoo-movement-convictions-charges
Schussler, D. (2006). Defining dispositions. Wading through murky waters. *The Teacher Educator, 41*(4), 251–268.
Smith, M. (Ed.) (2004). *Encyclopedia of rape*. Greenwood Press.
Stake, R. (2005). Qualitative case studies. In N. Denzin & Y. Lincoln (Eds.), *The SAGE handbook of qualitative research* (3rd ed.) (pp. 443-466). SAGE.
Stover, L., & Bach, J. (2011). Young adult literature as a call to social activism. In J. Hayn & J. Kaplan (Eds.), *Teaching young adult literature: Insights, considerations, and perspectives for the classroom teacher* (1st ed., pp. 203–222). Rowman & Littlefield.
Street, B. (1985). *Literacy in theory and practice*. Cambridge University Press.
Valenzuela, A. (1999). *Subtractive schooling: U.S.-Mexican youth and the politics of caring*. SUNY Press.
Vasquez, V., Stacie, L., Tate, S., & Harste, J. (Eds.). (2013). *Negotiating critical literacies with teachers: Theoretical foundations and pedagogical resources for pre-service and in-service contexts*. Routledge.
Villegas, A. (2007). Dispositions in teacher education: A look at social justice. *Journal of Teacher Education, 58*(5), 370–380.

Vygotsky, L. S. (1978). *Mind in society: The development of higher psychological processes* (M. Cole, V. John-Steiner, S. Scribner, & E. Souberman, Eds. &, Trans). Harvard University Press.

Wallin-Ruschman, J. (2014). A girl power study: Looking and listening to the role of emotions and relationality in developing critical consciousness. *Dissertations and Theses*, 1837.

Wellek, R., & Warren, A. (1949). *Theory of literature*. Harcourt Brace.

Zdilla, G. (2010). The appeal of young adult literature in late adolescence: College freshmen read YAL. In J. Alsup (Ed.), *Young adult literature and adolescent identity across cultures and classrooms* (pp. 191-203). Routledge.

The Anti-Hero: Using Media Representations of Gendered Violence to Negotiate Rape Culture, Suicide Intensity, and Neoliberal Belonging

Cameron Greensmith, Kennesaw State University, Adam Davies, University Guelph, and Jocelyn Sakal Froese, Wilfrid Laurier University

Introduction

Taylor Swift, an international pop star hailed by many anti-racist scholars, organizers, and activists as a 'white feminist' (Prins, 2022), is known for producing music and other new media around the topics of femininity, love, and girlhood—she was deemed the most streamed Spotify artist in 2023 (McAlister, 2023). Swift's various stages of her music career have been analyzed by gender, media, and cultural studies scholars for her depictions of girlhood, popular culture, romantic love, as well as power and agency (Chittenden, 2013; Prins, 2022). Her noted feud with Kanye West and Kim Kardashian, in which West used Swift's nude body in a sexually suggestive situation, came to a tipping point in his 2016 music video for his song, "Famous," leading to a reinvention for Swift upon her release of her 2017 album, *reputation* (Cullen, 2016)—many found West actions to be akin to sexual violence. *reputation*'s lead single, "Look What You Made Me Do," illustrated an empowered and agentic representation of Swift, with jabs at West, as well as her critics who might have positioned her as hypersexual and ingenuine. The figure of the snake, deployed generously throughout the music video for "Look What You Made Me Do," became a reclaimed image for Swift in response to online critics who described Swift using a snake emoji (Driessen, 2022)—referring to being a scoundrel, back stabber, or two-faced.

While witnessing and experiencing the realities of of misogyny, sexual violence, and rape culture, and well as general backlash from the public, Swift released her new album *Midnights*, in 2022 inspired by what keeps her up at night. In *Midnights*, Swift recorded and produced the song *Anti-Hero* to correct the public's perception of her, where she writes: "I should not be left to my own devices/ They come with prices and vices/ I end up in crisis (tale as old as time)/ I wake up screaming from dreaming." For the majority of Swift's musical career, she has been criticized by other musicians and the public despite being an incredibly successful artist. The song *Anti-Hero* is an ode to Swift's self: the lyrics contextualize this double-bind and constant negotiation of success through social filters of femininity, self-actualization, neoliberal individualism, and being 'too much.' By owning these 'flaws,' Swift calls attention to the internal and external persona of an *Anti-Hero* who is always under the watchful eye of the public.

Brown (2006) suggests that neoliberalism is

> "depict[ed through] free markets, free trade, and entrepreneurial rationality as achieved and normative, as promulgated through law and through social and economic policy—not simply as occurring by dint of nature... [Neoliberalism] produce[s] citizens as individual entrepreneurs and consumers whose moral autonomy is measured by their capacity for 'self-care'—their ability to provide for their own needs and service their own ambitions, whether as welfare recipients, medical patients, consumers of pharmaceuticals, university students, or workers in ephemeral occupations" (p. 694)

While queer, feminist, and girlhood studies scholars have engaged Swift's music and celebrity persona, less attention has been directed at Swift challenging or subverting gendered scripts through her evocation of the figure of the anti-hero—especially, within a culture that makes being a girl, within this neoliberal world, virtually impossible. This impossibility lies in the normalization and ritualization of rape culture: women and girls' bodies (including trans women and girls) experience and endure routine gendered and sexualized violence (Greensmith & Sakal Froese, 2021). This chapter explores the purpose of the figure of the anti-hero within the study of girlhood, when the suicidal or *mad* girl is centered. What purpose does the good life serve anti-hero girls? And, to paraphrase Swift, why do girls have to pay the price of survival and still experience crisis? Our chapter addresses how pedagogical strategies used by educators can sediment key learning from the HBO series *Euphoria* (the season two premier viewership hit 16 million in the United States alone [Mass, February 28, 2022]), which exposes the intersectional and violent impacts of rape culture, liveability, and girlhood.

In representations of girls within popular media, the figure of the supergirl and the anti-hero become salient representations that embody power in the form of agency or an unlikely heroine who critiques the status quo through her failure to perform unreasonable sanist and cisheteronormative societal expectations (Lethbridge, 2015). In this sense, both the supergirl and the anti-hero represent connected critiques of the patriarchal status quo; however, one (supergirl) offers a more binarized reading of empowered womanhood locked within the status quo. The other (anti-hero) illustrates a complex relationship between notions of agency, empowerment, and redefinitions of heroism and girlhood that seems to rub up against the status quo (Lethbridge, 2015).

An example of this can be considered in Vernon's (2018) analysis of heroism and womanhood in Hayao Miyazaki's film, *Princess Mononoke*. Vernon illustrates through her analysis of two female lead characters in Miyazaki's film, which explores themes of girlhood, agency, capitalism, and nature in feudal Japan, how the female lead characters of San and Lady Eboshi, while positioned differently, portray heroic productions of femininity and girlhood that are complicated by layers of independence, strength, and nurturance, as well as individual agency and community (Vernon, 2018). How girls and young women are positioned within gendered matrices offer room for more nuanced readings beyond simple binaries between subject positions of empowered and disempowered.

While empowering and powerful depictions of women and girls enter girls' media ecology (Lamb & Peterson, 2011; Murnen & Smolak, 2012)—the ever-expanding world in which young people find themselves that combines "technical, social, cultural, and place-based systems" (Ito et al., 2009, p. 31)—they routinely brush up against sexist and post-feminist constructions of girlhood. That is, girls are asked to negotiate competing discourses of success, likability, docility, and beauty, which are produced through neoliberal mechanisms of self-actualization. If girls are to survive within the existing social order that ritualized rape culture, their access to girlhood and the neoliberal 'good life' are often connection to notions of access, materialization, and empowerment (Greensmith & Sakal Froese, 2021). While notions of the neoliberal 'good life' might seemingly offer individual empowerment to girls who take on the supergirl, persona, this paper brings attention to the ways the 'good life' for girls requires the normalization of rape culture and forms of gendered violence (Greensmith & Sakal Froese, 2021).

As queer-identified scholars trained in girlhood studies, queer studies, and mad studies, we advocate for the critical importance of engaging with issues of gender-based violence and rape culture and feel passionately that pop culture and media offer opportune moments for discussions with and about young people and cisheteropatriarchal violence. Our chapter has two goals: 1) to explore the figure of the anti-hero and the supergirl as byproducts of rape culture and ask why educators seem to intervene at the individual rather than the systemic level; and 2) reexamine the figure of the anti-hero and supergirl within pedagogical contexts so to invite a radical rethinking of consent, rape culture, and suicide intensity (including suicide prevention) (Baril, 2022).

We explore the importance of reading and thinking with texts girls are engaging with to begin a dialogue surrounding consent, rape culture, and suicide intensity. We base our inquiry within the first two seasons of the HBO series *Euphoria*—a drama that centers on the protagonist Rue queer Black high school student who has experience with psychiatric institutions given their mental health diagnoses and substance use (alcohol, opioids, and other illicit substances). *Euphoria*, for many girls, highlights the intensity and complexity of their lives, provides an explicit critique of the cisheteropatriarchy that girls endure, and exposes the neoliberal good life as impossible to endure (Greensmith & Sakal Froese, 2021). We argue that *Euphoria* makes visible the power structures embedded in a culture that valorizes and ritualizes rape, highlighting the ways that youth and adults behave such as the white male-presenting, sexually confused character Nate whose violence comes from his queer father's socialization in the form of recklessness. While many of the characters endure the impacts and effects of rape culture and sexual violence, this chapter will focus on Nate as a figure of hyper-masculinity, Rue's friend Lexi as a supergirl figure, and Rue, as the anti-hero figure. Ultimately, we advocate that engaging with texts and media in a dialogical and transformative fashion (Freire, 1970) that might be challenging can provide an avenue for rich and meaningful conversations with students about the lived realities of girls and young women under cis-heteropatriarchal conditions.

Literature Review and Theoretical Framework

This project emerges from the scholarly and pedagogical contributions the authors have made in girlhood studies, queer studies, and mad studies where we have addressed the ways children and youth (including queer and trans girls) are required to live within and endure violence. We contend that texts, such as new media depictions of girlhood, gender, and violence, are products of contemporary culture and wrestle with current debates surrounding representation and rape culture—even if they do so in imperfect ways. Sakal Froese and Greensmith (2019) contend that adult anxieties of the text *13 Reasons Why* and its subsequent moral panic of youth and girls' experiences of madness does a disservice to young people themselves who articulate that these difficult texts open possibilities for *difficult* dialogue. Euphoria is yet another example of a text that young people engage in as it is created for young people (high schoolers and young adults) to consume and brings to the forefront the realities of gendered and sexual violence in girls' lives.

Girlhood studies as a theoretical framework provides this project with a multifaceted and multidisciplinary lens to examine how femininity and girlhood are produced in and through a rotating kaleidoscope of cultural expectations. To consider the constructs of the super girl and anti-hero, we first discuss the impacts of how these figures of girlhood are part of a larger neoliberal project that produces normative gendered and social expectations of life itself (Baril, 2022; Davies, 2023; Greensmith & Davies, 2017; Greensmith & Sakal Froese, 2018; 2021; Sakal Froese & Greensmith, 2019). Citing Berlant (2011) and Brown's (2006) work, Greensmith and Sakal Froese (2021) note "the pursuit of the good life has been undercut by neoliberal structures that insist on framing self-actualization in terms of capitalist production, value, and worth" (p. 87).

We build upon Berlant's (2011) queer/feminist critiques of the neoliberal good life to ask how certain girls, particularly the seemingly unattainable figure of the supergirl is deserving of intervention and care (Miller & Pencner, 2018; Pomerantz & Raby, 2017).

In a world that valorizes rape culture, the figure of the supergirl, produces success as attainable through hard work, achievement, and desire. Historically produced through popular culture and comics (Miller & Pencner, 2018), scholars contend that the figure of the supergirl is difficult to attain and imagined as a girl who is attractive *and* an academic (Pomerantz & Raby, 2017). In line with neoliberal articulations of girl power, the supergirl is produced in popular culture as heroine figures who use their lived experiences with gender inequality to 'fight back' while also maintaining the patriarchal status quo and nuclear family (Miller & Pencner, 2018). When girls fall outside of these unattainable scripts, they are produced as deviant, queer, or even an 'anti-hero'—which has been co-opted by Swift's empire.

To consider the figure of the anti-hero as a product of and resistance to Swifts' musical empire, we must consider the ways girl's lives are shaped by the pressures of living under what hooks (2000) calls "white supremacist capitalist patriarchy" (p. 4). The impacts of systematic violence on girls' livability is especially important in naming the inequalities produced in accessing the neoliberal good life. To experience the 'good life,' girls are required to maintain the status quo by being passive recipients, damsels in distress, or a sidekick; rarely ever a hero. Hagelin and Silverman (2022) note that for boys and men, the distinction between hero and 'anti-hero' is that the hero saves; the 'anti-hero' (in addition to being shrouded in ambiguity) "undercuts the common good" and if he does rescue the world "through intentional action … [he] lacks both noble purposefulness and the ability to create positive transformation" (p. 2). For women and girls, the available hero roles are pre-inscribed by their gender, not only because "women [and girls] are not expected to rescue society" but also because, instead "they are expected to showcase it, to demonstrate its values and commitments" (Hagelin & Silverman, 2022, p. 2). Thus, what becomes 'heroic' for women and girls simply means aligning with the status quo (e.g., maintaining the good life and all its expectations) in terms of feminine traits, including family roles.

The very act of rescuing or saving anything, then, becomes an anti-heroic action when performed by women and girls (Hagelin & Silverman, 2022, p. 3). Within this framework, any girl perceived to be putting pressure on the status quo becomes an anti-hero, but so too do otherwise heroic figures who exhibit non-feminine traits, such as Buffy from "Buffy the Vampire Slayer" (Hagelin & Silverman, 2022, p. 3), but also figures like Katniss Everdeen from the "Hunger Games." Lethbridge (2021) echoes this point, and directly ascribes the transformative possibility (from which men and boys as 'anti-heros' are precluded) to women and girls occupying the anti-hero role.' The author notes that "in terms of hero-politics then, the character does not so much represent a girl in the role of a typical male hero as offer a model that derives its strength from processes of transformation and mediation, arguably [of] stereotypically feminine traits" (Lethbridge, 2021, p. 99).

Lupold (2014) notes that films that center one form of the anti-hero—girl killers—feature both progressive and regressive elements which are further tied up with critiques of the sexualization of girls and young women in media. The girl anti-hero has transformed over time from 1) existing outside of conventional gender norms and the nuclear family, to 2) being framed through hypersexuality and delinquency, and 3) produced as "asexual yet extremely violent" (Lupold, 2014, p. 11). The 'anti-hero' avoids romantic and sexual partnership; instead, she picks up arms (or other means of violence) to protect herself, her family, and community. Lupold (2014) notices one pattern in the family structure that produces such anti-heros/girl killers: they tend to feature unreliable mothers (p. 17)—echoing Hagelin and Silverman (2022) contention that women and girls are meant to display cisheteropatriarchical values. Any deviation from the status quo becomes pathologized such that even when said deviations are mobilized towards the heroic, they are automatically figured as 'anti-heroes.'

Within Western culture, girls and women's dissent and refusals have been continually psychiatrized and classified as a form of illness and pathology (Ussher, 2017). Madness, often constructed as a state of mental, psychological, and emotional distress associated with a lack of 'reason' and self-control (Gomory & Dunleavy, 2017), is tied to and connected with women through harmful diagnoses, such as 'hysteria' and 'borderline personality disorder' (Ussher, 2017). Through this, the dissent and resistance of girls and women is commonly medicalized and deemed a pathology in need of psychiatric intervention and medical attention instead of a natural response to structural patriarchal conditions (Greensmith & Sakal Froese, 2018; 2021). It is no accident that the same actions taken up by women and girls may result in the actor being labeled as an anti-hero, as mad, or both under the restrictive framework of cisheteropatriarchy, as both labels work to undermine (at best) and to marginalize (at worst). We are interested in engaging with girls' and women's responses to harmful structural conditions as inherently pedagogical and worthy of engagement (Greensmith & Sakal Froese, 2018; 2021).

Euphoria: Representations of Gendered Violence and Rape Culture

The television series *Euphoria* engages with the lives of high school students in the fictional town of East Highland, California, as well as their experiences with substances, sexual violence, gender, and sexual identity, along with their interpersonal relationships and high school life. The series is narrated by Rue, portrayed by Zendaya—an actress who became famous through her starring role on the Disney Channel show, *Shake it Up* (Blue, 2017). Zendaya's movement from acting roles aimed for children on Disney towards more mature roles, given the themes of *Euphoria*, captured media attention upon the show's premiere. Thus, even the actress' acting trajectory experienced surveillance and regulation as she began to challenge her earlier Disney-fied image.

Nate Jacobs, who is played by Jacob Elordi, is the main antagonist in Euphoria. Nate is a vile figure of classism, toxic masculinity, and white cisheteronormative privilege. Throughout the two seasons, we are asked to engage Nate's character as a representation of misogyny and rape culture. Nate is a violent and unhinged character; we learn in season two that he is socialized into *becoming* a figure of toxic masculinity through the abuse he endures from his father (who is a representation of the nuclear family who, in turn, is secretive of his own queerness in service of protecting the status quo). In Nate's world, girls and women are presumed to be disposable and objects of desire. Early in season one, Nate produces himself as an alpha amongst his peer group; he spends a lot of his energy and time trying to convince his peers that Cassie (his then girlfriend Maddy's best friend) is a slut: "You fuck her like the whore she is and kick her ass to the curb" (Euphoria, Season 1).

The slut shaming of Cassie via Nate and the other boys' sharing of her sexually explicit photos seemingly legitimize her experiences of gendered and sexual violence in future episodes, rather than reading as an extreme violation of her privacy and dignity by her then-boyfriend McKay. Cassie is not the only character who experiences violence from Nate, as Maddy is violently raped by him—holding her head down as she says no. While Nate is portrayed as a figure of toxic masculinity and repulsive to the viewer, his actions mimic a snake where he slithers and slides from his violent actions. Importantly, while Nate does not shy away from sexism and other bad behaviors in public, his most violent actions happen in private, with himself and his target as the only witnesses (mirroring his father's secret sex life). His success in school is built off power, dominance, and fear—but he is not a hero, nor 'anti-hero.'

Diverging from Nate, although not entirely, is the character Lexi Howard, played by Maude Apatow, who aligns with the figure of the supergirl. Best friend to Rue, Lexi upholds the status quo in her desire to be and become successful.

Lexi recognizes Rue's struggles with mental health and addiction, and even when she notices that Rue is 'acting funny' or 'nodding off,' she does not intervene—for intervening would potentially mark Lexi as a target of misogyny, violence, and rape. Her post-feminist values are revealed to the viewer when she becomes a playwright of the script and performance "Our Life," which showcases her quiet observations of her close friend group in a theatrical and over-the-top performance.

To prop herself up as a supergirl, she needs to participate in rape culture, including by allowing attention directed at her sister, Cassie, to frame Cassie as being self-absorbed and sexually promiscuous. While Lexi can move outside of the shadows and into the center where everyone can see, she produces herself as creative, genuine, and intellectual, and her peer group as girls who cannot or are unwilling to fit themselves into the status quo. While Lexi may benefit from rape culture, she does not seem to be happy or content with the impact of her actions—she may never get access to the 'good life.' While she continues to be noticed as 'successful,' and take on the supergirl figure, she remains tied to the same sexist culture that Nate and other boys' benefit from. Though she can don a rosy facade, her commitments to the supergirl position mean that she is excluded from true liberation.

As the spiritual center of the show, Rue is one of the more complex characters. At some points Rue aligns with Nate and Lexi who take actions to reify rape culture and misogyny, and at other times she exists in opposition to the status quo. As a character, Rue's complexity as a queer Black high school student who struggles with mental health and addiction is worthy of a deeper exploration and deserves its own article. In this work, we contextualize Rue as an anti-hero. Viewers learn that life for Rue is painful after the loss of their father figure, and her in home experiences with his slow death, the family's difficulty navigating the costs of death and dying in the context of a for-profit health care system, and the high dose opiate medications that come as part of the experience shape Rue's possible becomings. It is no surprise that as a teenager, Rue engages in reckless behaviors and even develops an addiction—all of which bring attention to the impossibilities of the 'good life.' By being unpredictable, Rue's character is shown to be unhinged, reified through her experiences with madness: she is self-sabotaging, difficult to count on, relapses often, and is represented as a cheater. It would be easy to align the characters of Rue and Nate; however, if we think of Rue as an anti-hero, we can lean into her experience to name and ultimately disrupt the unlivable conditions of the neoliberal good life. In other words, Rue's defiance of social acceptability and the status quo is commentary on the violence that suicidal or mad girls endure.

Being an anti-hero exists beyond Swift framings of girlhood as defiant under neoliberalism; Rue's evocations of the anti-hero provide educators with the capacity to resist pathologizing rhetoric that seemingly blames Rue for not participating in the normalizing apparatus of misogyny, cisheteropatriarchy, and rape culture. The ways that Rue imperfectly intervenes into the status quo by disrupting the nuclear family and the expectations placed upon queer girls to conform make those very things visible: her disruptions—including those that ultimately harm herself most of all—act as a light that illuminates the interstice at which all of *Euphoria's* characters are expected to survive: in a post-9/11 world marked by the intensification of neoliberalism at both registers: the profit-driven capitalist register, and the cut-throat systems of hierarchy (white supremacism and patriarchy) that together seek to marginalize, shrink, intoxicate, incapacitate, and mock. All the actions Rue takes direct the viewer's attention at the impossibilities of living within a neoliberal regime that makes living through pain and loss unbearable. There are moments where we see Rue develop as a character—they fall in and out of love, connect with their sister, and find a sponsor. However, most of the energy Rue puts out into the world is, like Jessica in *13 Reasons Why*, a form of what Berlant (2007) calls slow death, specifically "sentience, without full intentionality" (p. 759).

Making Youth Texts Matter: Pedagogical Implications

We end the chapter by situating the figure of the anti-hero within the lexicon of critical pedagogy (Freire, 1970) to equip educators in engaging young people on the topic of consent, rape, and suicide intensity. We end this section with some recommendations illustrating how teachers might use these and other *difficult* texts to inspire change and address the sexism girls seem to be required to endure to get access to the good life. Despite calls to depoliticize education and critical thinking, in the case of book banning's across the United States (Sakal Froese & Greensmith, 2019), and policies that resist what teachers can and cannot do (such as Georgia's HB1074 passed in 2022 banning educators K-12 educators from teaching about 'divisive concepts' related to race and representation in the United States).

Teachers and administrators, operating under these restrictions, are posed with unique challenges, given that there are increasing pressures to conform to the status quo and social pressures to 'teach to test.' One way to combat these mechanisms of social control that are limiting teachers' capacity to teach and dialogue about social justice and embed these conversations and critiques of sexism, misogyny, and rape culture into the assignments and learning objectives offered to students. For example, as part of the Georgia Social Science 'Standards of Excellence,' students are to "C1c: explain culture as an organizing tool in society" and "C1d: describe the components of culture to include language, symbols, norms, and values" (Georgia Department of Education, 2016). Teachers can use the standards of excellence and build out content and assignments that address the complex cultural and social phenomena in television and provide *Euphoria* (as well as other texts that offer complex intersectional critique) as an option to write assignments, present findings, complete online discussion posts, and dialogue in class.

We call on all educators and other helping professionals working with girls to take their experiences of sexism, experiences with race and rape culture, and suicide intensity seriously by having meaningful conversations with them—one of which can find a root in *Euphoria* as text. Dialogue can occur in formal and informal capacities whereby teachers discuss at the beginning of class if students have watched the most recent episode and if they have any insights on how they felt or what they learned. These conversations can then be used to help pivot the students into participating in 'words that hurt' or 'invisible backpack privilege' exercise and using the text to help students write poetry or music around a theme discussed. While we offer some recommendations, we resit offering specifics, given that queer theories center disruption and mess. Conscious-raising, we believe, is the first opportunity for teachers to begin utilizing *Euphoria* in their classrooms. Wink (2011) notes how: "The philosophy that supports transformative teaching and learning is founded on the principles that theory and practice are joined to form praxis. Not only must democracy be taught; it must be lived within the classroom, the school, and the community" (p. 144). Pragmatically, we hope that these critiques and engagements with texts youth and girls engage will serve as a catalyst for social change—especially in provinces and states across Canada and the United States banning certain kinds of discussions and identities from entering the classroom (Alexander, 2024; *The Southerner* Editorial Board, 2023; Lobosco, 2023; Sakal Froese & Greensmith, 2019).

What constitutes a 'text' is a fluid concept, as television shows, films, and graphic novels offer extensive pedagogical possibilities for engaging with youth about concepts pertaining to social justice. These texts offer transformative pedagogical opportunities for challenging the hierarchies that socialize students into normalization and social obedience (Torres, 2003). Engaging with *Euphoria* and the figure of Rue as an anti-hero that challenges neoliberal hegemony provides students an opportunity to engage with students and young people about the patriarchal structural conditions that girls, such as Rue, live within through transformative teaching, including: 1) develop an exercise about contemporary poetry and music lyrics, looking at Lil Nas X and Taylor Swift; 2) organize a field trip to the local human rights museum to discuss history, action, and coalition building; or, 3) have students watch or rewatch *Euphoria* and assess the first seasons plot and character development.

While producers of shows, such as *Euphoria* or even *13 Reasons Why*, might engage with issues of illicit drug use and suicidality, there is still more work to be done to engage viewers with conversations of rape and rape culture, as well as how patriarchal systems and societies might impact the daily lives of young women and girls (Greensmith & Sakal Froese, 2021). Exploring the figures of the supergirl and the anti-hero provide avenue to explore how neoliberal fictions of post-feminist times continue to mask the girls' and young women's experiences with violence and mental distress as they are marked by neoliberal economies as either 'failures' or 'successes' (Greensmith & Sakal Froese, 2021). By examining media and texts with students that are challenging, educators can engage with students - especially girls and young women—about their daily realities living under patriarchal societies. As Freire (1970) notes, instead of avoiding challenging—or even 'radical'— conversations with students, "On the contrary, the more radical the person is, the more fully [they] enter into reality so that, knowing it better, [they] can better transform it" (Freire, 1970, p. 39). We advocate that part of a transformative approach to teaching and learning is engaging with media and texts that illustrate challenging and difficult realities over avoiding and banning such examples.

References

Alexander, C. (2024, Feb 22). Georgia school board upholds firing of cobb teacher for reading controversial book. *Atlanta Journal of Constitution*. https://www.ajc.com/education/georgia-board-upholds-firing-of-cobb-teacher-for-reading-controversial-book/Z4D5CUX4ERD7HG7ZK77XILOR5M/

Baril, A. (2023). *Undoing suicidism: A trans, queer, crip approach to rethinking (assisted) suicide*. Temple University Press.

Berlant, L. (2011). *Cruel optimism*. Duke University Press.

Berlant, L. (2007). Slow death (sovereignty, obesity, lateral agency). *Critical Inquiry*, *33*(4), 754-780.

Blue, M. G. (2017). *Girlhood on Disney Channel: Branding, celebrity, and femininity*. Taylor & Francis.

Brown, W. (2006). American nightmare: Neoliberalism, neoconservatism, and de-democratization. *Political Theory*, *34*(6), 690-714.

Chittenden, T. (2013). In my rearview mirror: Female teens' prospective remembering of future romantic relationships through the lyrics in Taylor Swift songs. *Journal of Children and Media*, *7*(2), 186-200.

Cullen, S. (2016). The innocent and the runaway: Kanye West, Taylor Swift, and the cultural politics of racial melodrama. *Journal of popular music studies*, *28*(1), 33-50.

Davies, A. W. (2023). Maddening pre-service early childhood education and care through poetics: Dismantling epistemic injustice through mad autobiographical poetics. *Contemporary Issues in Early Childhood*, *24*(2), 124-146.

Driessen, S. (2022). Look what you made them do: Understanding fans' affective responses to Taylor Swift's political coming-out. *Celebrity Studies*, *13*(1), 93-96.

Dubrofsky, R. E. (2016). A vernacular of surveillance: Taylor Swift and Miley Cyrus perform white authenticity. *Surveillance & Society*, *14*(2), 184-196.

The Southerner Editorial Board. (2023, Sep 5). Florida ban of AP classes censors valuable race, gender teachings. *The Southerner*. https://thesoutherneronline.com/92774/comment/florida-ban-of-ap-classes-censors-valuable-race-and-gender-teachings/

Freire, P. (1970). *Pedagogy of the oppressed*. Bloomsbury Publishing USA.

Freire, P. (1983). The importance of the act of reading. *Journal of education*, *165*(1), 5-11.

Georgia Department of Education. (2016). Sociology—Social Studies Georgia Standards of Excellence. *Georgia Department of Education*. https://lor2.gadoe.org/gadoe/file/39a68ada-5e37-4c02-8f0e-1baa0ecd12e7/1/Social-Studies-Sociology-Georgia-Standards.pdf

Gomory, T., & Dunleavy, D. J. (2017). Madness: A critical history of "mental health care" in the United States. In B. M. Z. Cohen (Ed.), *Routledge international handbook of critical mental health* (pp. 117–125). Routledge.

Greensmith, C., & Davies, A. (2017). Queer and trans at school: Gay–straight alliances and the politics of inclusion. In Chen, X., Raby, R., & Albanese, P (Eds.), *The sociology of childhood and youth studies in canada: categories, inequalities, engagement.* (pp. 314 – 331). Canadian Scholars Press.

Greensmith, C., & Sakal Froese, J. (2021). Fantasies of the good life: Responding to rape culture in *13 Reasons Why*. *Girlhood Studies*, *14*(1), 85-100.

Greensmith, C., Sakal Froese, J. (2018). Glorifying suicide?: Radical encounters with difficult texts, radical approaches to youth care. *CYC-Online*, *235*, 70-78.

Hagelin, Sarah, Silverman, Gillian. (2022). *The new female anti-hero: The disruptive women of twenty-first-century television*. University of Chicago Press.

hooks b. (1994) *Teaching to transgress: Education as the practice of freedom*. Routledge.

hooks, b. (2000). *Feminism is for everybody: Passionate politics*. South End Press.

Ito, M., Baumer, S., Bittanti, M., & Cody, R. (2009). *Hanging out, messing around, and geeking out: Kids living and learning with new media*. MIT press.

Lamb, S., & Peterson, Z. D. (2011). Adolescent girls' sexual empowerment: Two feminists explore the concept. *Sex Roles*.

Lethbridge, Stefanie. (2015). Antihero, hero, *Hunger Games*. *E-Journal zu Kulturen des Heroischen*, 3(1), 93-103.

Lobosco, K. (2023, May 27). New Iowa law restricts gender identity education, bans books with sexual content. *CNN*. https://www.cnn.com/2023/05/27/politics/iowa-law-gender-identity-book-ban/index.html

Lupold, E. (2014). Adolescence in action: Screening narratives of girl killers. *Journal of Girlhood Studies*, 7(2), 6-24.

Mass, J. (2022, Feb 28). 'Euphoria' is now HBO's second-most watched show behind 'Game of Thrones.' *Variety*. https://variety.com/2022/tv/news/euphoria-season-2-finale-ratings-1235192015/

McAlister, I. (2023, Dec 1). It's a wrap! Taylor Swift crowned 2023's most-streamed artist. *CBC Kids News*. https://www.cbc.ca/kidsnews/post/its-a-wrap-taylor-swift-crowned-2023s-most-streamed-artist#:~:text=It's%20official%3A%20Taylor%20Swift%20is,billion%20times%20globally%20since%20Jan.

Miller, K. L., & Plencner, J. (2018). Supergirl and the corporate articulation of neoliberal feminism. *New Political Science*, 40(1), 51-69.

Murnen, S. K., & Smolak, L. (2012). Social considerations related to adolescent girls' sexual empowerment: A response to Lamb and Peterson. *Sex roles*, 66, 725-735.

Pomerantz, S., & Raby, R. (2017). *Smart girls: Success, school, and the myth of post-feminism*. University of California Press.

Prins, A. (2022). On good girls and woke white women: Miss Americana and the performance of popular white womanhood. *Celebrity Studies*, 13(1), 102-107.

Sakal Froese, J., & Greensmith, C. (2019). Que(e)rying youth suicide: Sexism, racism, and violence in *Skim* and *Thirteen Reasons Why*. *Cultural Studies Review*, 25(2), 31-51.

Torres, C. A. (2003). Paulo Freire, education and transformative social justice learning. In C. Wiessner, S. Meyer, N. Pfhal, & P. Neaman (Eds.), *Transformative learning in action: Building bridges across contexts and disciplines; Proceeding of the 5th International Conference on Transformative Learning* (pp. 443–446). Teachers College

Ussher, J. M. (2017). A critical feminist analysis of madness: Pathologising femininity through psychiatric discourse. In B. Cohen (Ed.), *Routledge international handbook of critical mental health* (pp. 72-78). Routledge.

Vernon, A. (2018). Beyond girlhood in Ghibli: mapping heroine development against the adult anti-hero in *Princess Mononoke*. In R. Denison (Ed.), *Princess Mononoke: Understanding Studio Ghibli's monster princess* (pp. 115–130). Bloomsbury.

Wink, J. (2011). *Critical pedagogy: Notes from the real world*. Pearson/Allyn & Bacon.

Notes on Contributors

Volume Editors
Kathleen Colantonio-Yurko is an associate professor of literacy education at SUNY Brockport. Her research interests include young adult literature, third culture kids, and topics related to adolescent literacy. She has been published in journals such as *ALAN, Journal of Literacy Research*; *Journal of Language and Literacy Education;* and *Study and Scrutiny: Research on Young Adult Literature*.

Brittany Adams is an assistant professor of literacy education at the University of Alabama. Her research interests include critical literacy, children's and young adult literature, and the preparation of culturally sustaining teachers. Her work has been published in *Journal of Literacy Research*; *The Reading Teacher*; *Literacy Research and Instruction*; and *Literacy Research: Theory, Method, and Practice*.

Foreword Author
Ashley S. Boyd is a professor of English/English education at Washington State University where she teaches graduate courses on critical and cultural theory and undergraduate courses on English Methods and Young Adult Literature. A former secondary English language arts teacher, Ashley's current scholarship examines practicing teachers' social justice pedagogies and their critical content knowledge and explores how young adult literature is an avenue for cultivating students' critical literacies.

Chapter Authors
Shelby Boehm is an assistant professor of English education at Illinois State University. Prior to this role, she taught high school English in Florida. Her scholarship considering the democratic possibilities of secondary English classrooms has been published in journals such as *English Journal, The ALAN Review,* and *Study and Scrutiny: Research on Young Adult Literature*.

NOTES ON CONTRIBUTORS

Adam Davies is an assistant professor of sexualities, genders, and social change at the University of Guelph in Guelph, Canada. They hold a PhD in Curriculum Studies and Teacher Development and Sexual Diversity Studies from the Ontario Institute for Studies in Education at the University of Toronto. Adam's research areas are critical masculinity studies, queer theory, LGBTQ studies in education, sexuality education and sexual health, and critical disability studies.

Molly C. Driessen is an assistant professor of social work at Providence College. Her research is focused on issues pertaining to intimate partner and sexual violence, specifically campus sexual assault, as well as issues related to student well-being and trauma, broadly. She teaches social work courses and maintains a part-time clinical practice.

Cameron Greensmith is an associate professor in the Department of Social Work and Human Services at Kennesaw State University. Dr. Greensmith researches the ways systems and structures of power and inequality impact helping professions, such as higher education, non-profits, and clinical social work. Their research utilizes anti-racist, anti-colonial, and queer perspectives to investigate the ways helping professionals develop relationships with and support marginalized youth, adults, and communities, as well as how neoliberal notions of professionalism promote exclusionary logics and systemic oppression.

Melanie Hundley is a professor in the practice of English education at Vanderbilt University's Peabody College. She teaches writing methods courses that focus on digital and multimodal composition and young adult literature courses that explore race, class, gender, and sexual identity in young adult texts. Her research and work on young adult literature has been published widely across numerous journals. She is past editor of *The ALAN Review*.

Mark A. Lewis is a professor of literacy education at James Madison University. He has over 30 publications, including multiple book chapters and in scholarly journals such as *English Education, English Journal, Middle Grades Research Journal, Study & Scrutiny, The ALAN Review, Journal of Literacy Research,* and *Reading Research Quarterly*. He is also a co-author of *Reading the World through Sports and Young Adult Literature* and *Rethinking the "Adolescent" in Adolescent Literacy*.

Elizabeth A. Marshall is an associate professor at Simon Fraser University. An interdisciplinary scholar interested in childhood and popular culture, she is the author of *The Drinking Curriculum: A Cultural History of Childhood and Alcohol, Graphic Girlhoods: Visualizing Education and Violence*, co-author with

Leigh Gilmore of *Witnessing Girlhood*, and editor of *Rethinking Popular Culture and Media*. Marshall's articles have appeared in numerous journals, including *Feminist Media Studies*, *Rethinking Schools*, *Language Arts*, and *Women's Studies Quarterly*.

Gillian E. Mertens is an assistant professor of literacy education at SUNY Cortland and a former middle school English Language Arts teacher from central Florida. Her research interests include critical digital and information literacies, identity-focused teacher preparation, and the interplay between the Internet and identity. Her scholarship has been published in journals such as *Reading Research Quarterly*, *Middle School Journal*, *Journal of Research on Technology in Education*, and *Research in the Teaching of English*.

Henry "Cody" Miller is an associate professor of English education in the Department of Education and Human Development at SUNY Brockport. Prior to that role, he taught high school English in Florida for seven years. His research and teaching focus on young adult literature, LGBTQ curriculum, and graphic novels.

Amber Moore is an assistant professor of teaching with the Department of Language and Literacy Education at The University of British Columbia. Her research interests include: adolescent literacies; arts-based research; English education; feminist pedagogies; teacher and teacher librarian education; rape culture; and representations of youth in popular culture and YA literature. Her scholarship can be found across a number of publications such as *English Journal*, *Feminist Media Studies*, *Journal of Adolescent and Adult Literacy*, and *New Review of Children's Literature and Librarianship*.

Michael Neel is a coach, facilitator, and scholar who works with leaders in learning organizations to support leading in learning and flourishing. His teaching and scholarly interests focus on professional learning and on the intersection of policy and practice in learning settings. In addition to his faculty role at Vanderbilt University, Michael provides leadership coaching.

Jie Park is an associate professor of education at Clark University. A language and literacy scholar, she studies immigrant youth and their literacy and language practices in out-of-school and school-based settings. Her most recent work has been published in *Anthropology and Education Quarterly*, the *Journal of Adolescent and Adult Literacy*, *English Education*, and the *International Journal of Multicultural Education*.

NOTES ON CONTRIBUTORS

Emily Pendergrass is an associate professor of literacy at Vanderbilt University where she works with teachers to develop their expertise as future literacy coaches and reading specialists as the director of the Reading Education Program. Her research interests revolve around the complexities of teaching readers who struggle with school-based texts and using new literacies in middle school classrooms.

Kathryn Pendergrass is a student at Lewis and Clark College majoring in biology with a data science minor. She is currently interested in how organisms interact with each other and their environment and is looking to pursue a graduate degree in ecology. When not studying, you can find her outside with her dog, dancing West Coast Swing, or creating visual arts.

Luke Rodesiler is a professor of secondary education at Purdue University Fort Wayne. His work has appeared in refereed journals that include *English Education*, *English Journal*, and *The ALAN Review*, among others. He is also a co-author of *Reading the World through Sports and Young Adult Literature*, the author of *Bringing Sports Culture to the English Classroom*, and a co-editor of *Developing Contemporary Literacies through Sports*.

Jocelyn Sakal Froese teaches at Wilfrid Laurier University, in the Departments of English and Film Studies and Brantford Foundations. Their research looks at queer and queered representations in comics and visual media.

Lorelei Starkey is a senior undergraduate student majoring in English education at Illinois State University. After graduating, she plans to continue her commitment to teaching and learning by obtaining a master's degree in English education. During her time as an undergraduate student, she was president of a Registered Student Organization focused on advocating for sexual assault survivors and helping victims of violence have accessible resources.

Made in the USA
Monee, IL
28 April 2026